WORKING MEN'S COLLEGE

LIBRARY REGULATIONS

The Library is open every week-day evening (except Saturday), from 6.30 to 9.30 p.m.

This book may be kept for three weeks. If not returned within that period, the borrower will be liable to a fine of 2np per week.

If lost or damaged, the borrower will be required to make good such loss or damage.

Up to three books may be borrowed at a time at the discretion of the Librarian.

HISTORY

An Introduction for the Intending Student

CONTRIBUTORS

Harold Perkin

Michael Argles

John Creed

Anthony Tuck

Austin Woolrych

David Hamer

John Marshall

Clive Church

Michael Heale

Martin Blinkhorn

John MacKenzie

Robert Fox

HISTORY

An Introduction for the Intending Student

Edited by

Harold Perkin

Professor of Social History,
University of Lancaster

LONDON
ROUTLEDGE & KEGAN PAUL

First published 1970
by Routledge & Kegan Paul Ltd
Broadway House, 68–74 Carter Lane
London E.C.4
Printed in Great Britain
by Willmer Brothers Limited
Birkenhead, Cheshire
© *Routledge & Kegan Paul Ltd 1970*
ISBN 0 7100 6814 X (C)
ISBN 0 7100 6815 8 (P)

CONTENTS

v

PREFACE

Of all the subjects taught in universities and colleges, history, it might well be argued, least needs an introduction for the intending student. No-one can get through any kind of school without some exposure to it in one form or another, and everyone knows, or thinks he knows, what it is about. And yet from the remarks one hears not only from intending students and members of the public but also from one's own colleagues in other disciplines within the university it is clear that there is a great deal of misunderstanding of what history at the university is about, how we do it and with what purposes, academic and vocational. There is equally a failure to realize how many different kinds of history can be studied at the university, either in honours history degrees or in association with other disciplines. The aim of this book is to give some insight into the range of different subject matters, as wide as the whole range of human experience, covered by the term history, and to explore briefly the aims, sources and methods, as well as the pleasures and uses, of some of those most frequently studied in universities and colleges.

There are, of course, omissions, among them pre-history, art history, 'cultural history', the history of ideas, industrial archaeology, and some others, though most of these are mentioned under other headings in the course of the book. The reason is that it was thought better for the sake of unity of tone and approach to invite contributors from one university which happens to study a wide range of different kinds of history and let each of them describe his own approach to his subject rather than to pursue a more diffuse comprehensiveness. All the authors except two belong or, in the case of Dr David Hamer, recently belonged to the Depart-

PREFACE

ment of History of the University of Lancaster, while the remaining two belong to the Department of Classics and the University Library. All of us, however, have experience of one or more other universities, and we have tried to take a universal rather than a parochial point of view. If here and there we have inadvertently failed we sincerely apologize to our colleagues in other universities and colleges, to whom this book is respectfully, though without permission, dedicated.

HAROLD PERKIN

I

The Uses of History

Harold Perkin

'What is the use of history?' That is a question you often hear from people, even people in universities, who think there is no answer to it. 'That's past history,' the same people tend to say when they mean something that is dead and gone and no longer relevant. History in the immortal words of *1066 and All That* is 'What you can remember', and what most people can remember from their schooldays is a jumble of facts about kings, parliaments and battles which, even when they are correct, have little relevance outside a television quiz. Fortunately, school history is changing and now often deals in a more illuminating way with more interesting themes, but then what is the use of it beyond the pleasure it gives to amateur historians and the money it earns for professional ones? And why go on with it at the university when there are so many more modern and 'relevant' subjects to study?

Well, pleasure has its uses, too, and most of the contributors to this volume will tell you of the pleasure and delight their own particular brand of historical study has given to them. 'History' comes from a Latin word for a story, which comes from a Greek word for an enquiry, and there is a special kind of pleasure from seeing 'what happened next', especially if the story is true rather than fictional, and a special kind of delight in enquiring and finding out for yourself, especially something which no-one living today has found out before. 'History for its own sake', as a pleasurable hobby or pastime, like literature, art, science, sport or

1

almost anything else, needs no defence. If you like it, and increasing numbers of people with no professional interest in it do, then you do it, and no-one has any right to question, as long as you do it in your own time. But there is the rub: why should anyone be paid to do it by someone else, by their parents or the taxpayer? What is the use of history to society or the State? What is the use of it to you yourself in your post-university life and career?

The answer is that history has many uses, from the very widest, that it is all around us and we cannot escape it, to the narrowest, that unless we know how a particular event came to happen we cannot begin to know what is likely to happen next. On the broadest front, we are all of us faced with the question of Milton's Adam, 'How came I thus, how here?' Seen through the lens of a snapshot camera the world of the instant present is a puzzling place. 'The moving finger writes and, having writ, moves on' but, contrary to Omar Khayyam, immediately cancels most of the line, leaving only the merest traces of evidence of what has happened in the permanent records of what immediately becomes the past. Anyone 'born yesterday', without experience of more than today's world, is at a complete loss to understand it, to 'know the ropes' and how they came to tie themselves in such complicated knots. To ask in this situation 'What is the use of history?' is like asking 'What is the use of experience?' History is the summarized experience of society, as experience is the condensed history of the individual. Without experience the individual is as lost as a baby without a mother, a learner driver without a qualified passenger, a potholer without a torch. Without history a society scarcely exists, since it inheres only in the continuing relationships between its members, which in turn are merely the expectations that certain patterns of conduct and mutual service will continue in the future as they did in the past; and if these patterns of conduct change, as they do in response to altered circumstances such as war, economic crises, population growth, the impact of new ideas, and the like, they do so not in a random or arbitrary manner but within certain limits of possibility which an experienced observer or a well-informed historian will recognize. The experienced observer will know this intuitively, if his experience goes back far enough: the well-informed historian will know it consciously and systematically, because it is his job to find out and present it coherently.

Let us take, for example, the question of whether or not Britain should join the European Economic Community. The inexperienced observer will listen to the politicians' arguments, and will tend to think that it is merely a question of balancing economic gains and losses. But the historian will know it is much more than that, that there is a long history behind the Common Market going back to the German *Zollverein* of 1834 and the Prussian Maassen Tariff of 1818, and even to Napoleon's dissolution of the Holy Roman Empire and the 'rationalization' of Germany at the Congress of Vienna. From this he will know that common markets, if successful, commonly lead to closer political union, under the leadership of the dominant partner or partners. He will also know, from this and other examples, that common markets do not benefit all the partners equally, even at the economic level. Ireland was in a common market with Britain at the time of the Famine, the Southern States of America with the Northern after the Civil War, Sicily with northern Italy today. It all depends, he will know, on the political terms of the union and the economic competitiveness of the regional partners. Whether he will still be able to make a decision under the weight of so much knowledge—or knowing what the unknowable factors are—is an open question, but at least he will make it with his eyes open, and will also be able to make a better decision in the sense of knowing what ought to go into the treaty.

Or take the question of immigration into this country. The inexperienced observer may think that it is merely a question of liberal principles versus colour prejudice. But the well-informed historian will know that there are many complex factors involved, that on the one hand countries that have sealed their gates against newcomers have cut themselves off from new ideas, valuable skills, much-needed labour,

3

but on the other that every country in the world has had to set some limit to the influx of newcomers, especially those from different and not easily assimilable cultures— how much happier, to take a non-coloured example, the United States would have been without the immigration of Sicilian Mafiosi!—and too much cheap labour can, as Irish labour nearly did in some areas of Britain in the last century, undermine wages and the living standard of the mass of the people. Again, a knowledge of history does not make for an easy answer, but at least it makes possible a necessary distinction between those politicians who are genuinely seeking a solution and those who are cynically using popular prejudice to ride into power.

Professor Trevor-Roper in a recent paper to the London School of Economics even talks of history 'taking its revenge' on nations and individuals who have neglected it, and gives the example of the 'historic nations' in the nineteenth century—the Poles, Italians and Germans—leading the revolt against the anti-historical, cosmopolitan, international men and ideas of the eighteenth-century 'enlightenment'. He further suggests that a knowledge of the Wars of the Roses can throw much light on the war in Vietnam, and a knowledge of the co-existence of Christendom and the Turkish Empire on the present confrontation between East and West. And he warns against accepting at face value contemporary ideological interpretations of such events as the Spanish Civil War or the rise of Hitler, which can be interpreted and understood only against the background of the detailed history of Spanish or German society over several generations. ('The Past and the Present: History and Sociology', *Past and Present,* No. 42, February 1969.)

All this illustrates the use of history at the most general level, to the citizen and voter trying to understand and take his own small share in the political decisions which concern us all. It suggests that history should be taught to everyone as part of their general education for life so that they can better understand the world they live in. But why should some people go further, and specialize in it at university level? One obvious answer is, so that they can teach the rest what they need to know. This is a good answer, as far as it goes. Unless some people study it full-time and professionally how can anyone teach it properly? Such specialists, if they are properly trained, will not make the mistake of considering themselves superior citizens, better able to make up their minds on the major political issues of the day. On the contrary, they will know how complex those issues are and, in so far as they are concerned at all with current affairs, will see it as their task to avoid glib answers and to lay out the full range of factors which affect a given issue, leaving the decision to be made by the individual according to his own moral criteria and political preferences. But their main task will be simply to teach history, the history of any period, without any preoccupation with its direct bearing on the present day. Teleological history, subordinated that is to the immediate need to arrive at and explain the present—the end literally dictating the means—is inevitably bad history, since it does not allow the past to have its own concerns, values or prejudices, and so inevitably distorts it. Moreover—and this is what undermines it with its own excavator—it fails in the very task it sets itself: unless the history of any time and place is studied 'straight', in its own terms and for its own interest, it does not yield up whatever lessons, in the way of exemplifying how things really happen, it is capable of giving to the present. In other words, historians teach best and most relevantly when they teach what they know about the periods and places they have studied, and let their hearers draw their own conclusions about how to apply the 'lessons of history' to contemporary affairs. If they do the job well enough they will so enlarge the experience of their audience that the latter cannot fail to set current affairs in a larger and more objective context.

Much of that context, nevertheless, will consist of the history of our own society. This is the justification for giving the potential teachers of history in this country, as all history departments and faculties do, a thorough grounding in British history. Without some notion of where we, the British, came from in historical time and have arrived at in the historic (i.e. continuing) present, we cannot place ourselves

5

in the wide ocean of space-time, and navigate accordingly. This is true of all aspects of our history, whether political, social, economic, intellectual, aesthetic or any other. For some historians like Professor G. R. Elton history is primarily 'the history of government in its widest sense', and if we allow that politics is simply those issues which we as a society wish to dispute in public, this is often nearly true. Many of the issues in political dispute are social or economic, religious or moral, educational or scientific, ideological or aesthetic; amongst recent ones, the new social security system, the national incomes policy, scientology, cannabis, the public schools commission, heart transplants and the legal definition of death, student anarchism and 'the revolution within the revolution', or Miss Jennie Lee's patronage of the arts. There is no aspect of human conduct or preferences which is not potentially political: sumptuary laws in Elizabethan England or Mao's China, sexual relations outside marriage in California or inside marriage in South Africa, the right to strike in Mrs Castle's Britain or Mr Brezhnev's Russia.

There are some issues, however, which are more purely political than others, notably the history of government in its narrower sense of the actual struggle for power amongst politicians, the development of the constitution and the changing structure of administration. These are so important that they take up, along with the dominant issues in political dispute from time to time, a large part of the study of history in all universities. British government in both the wider and the narrower senses is soaked in history. More than most it is evolutionary government, its unwritten constitution the continuously changing product of history, Scottish and English law basically customary, the Common Law as amended and enlarged by statute, central and local administration the product of no code and subject to no *droit administratif,* its procedures, conventions and even its personnel explicable only in the light of history. The role and purpose of political history, especially British political history, at the university will be discussed in various chapters below, notably by Dr Tuck,

6

Professor Woolrych and Dr Hamer in Chapters 4, 5 and 6.

History, however, is about the whole life of man in past society, and there are important aspects of man's life which, while potentially political, are not continuously so. For this reason other kinds of history have come into existence, to compensate for the neglect of these aspects by traditional political historians. Ideally, of course, the historian should deal with every aspect of his chosen society. In most universities, however, the balance has to be redressed by teaching non-political history in separate courses and sometimes even separate departments, notably social and/or economic history. The late R. H. Tawney argued more than forty years ago, as a member of the Hadow Committee which first recommended secondary education for all, that all children should be taught this kind of history since it had most relevance to their life and work when they left school. Economic history deals with how men in the past earned their livings, produced goods and services, shared out the proceeds, and exchanged their shares or part of them for the other things they desired. Without production, distribution and exchange of the means of life no other human activity would be possible: no politics, no government, no wars, no crime, no religion, no literature, no art, no sports or pastimes, no thought or action of any kind. Political history obviously has to deal with the sinews of government and war, the taxable capacity of the population, industrial and commercial policy, and so on, but unless it is some historian's job to treat the economy and its development systematically they will only be dealt with incidentally and thus in a misleading and unenlightening way. Economic history also requires at least an elementary understanding of technology, including agricultural techniques as well as industrial and transport history. In some universities this has led to an emphasis on industrial archaeology, the study of technology through the actual machines, factories, civil engineering works and so on which have survived from the past, but this is perhaps best considered in relation to local and regional history, below. A full understanding of

7

technology may require a knowledge of science, but the history of science, a growing interest in some universities, is a separate study, related to the history of ideas and philosophy, and is dealt with separately by Dr Fox in Chapter 13.

Social history is studied in most universities alongside and in the same courses as economic history. It deals, first of all, with the way men in the past have used their political power and economic resources to live their lives, pass their time, enjoy themselves—or not, as the case may be—and the conditions in which they have done so. But it goes deeper than that: just as the economic historian must deal systematically with the development of the economy as a whole, so the social historian must deal with the development of society as a whole, that is with the changing system of relationships between its members which we call the social structure. The social structure of any society is indispensable to an understanding of its political life and economic activity, but unless some historian specializes in it it tends to get neglected or treated as a peripheral matter.

The importance of social and economic history for an understanding of the modern world, with its population explosion, its growing gap between the rich industrial nations and the poor agrarian ones, its split between East and West over how society and the economy should be organized, and its growing problem of race relations, is self-evident, and the teacher of history must obviously be equipped to deal with it. What is perhaps less evident is the need for historical understanding of our world at a much humbler level, in the local environment of our own immediate community. In spite of cars and aeroplanes, radio and television, we all spend a large part of our lives in the strictly local environment of our own village, suburb, town or city. This indeed is where history impinges upon us most, for the very fields and footpaths, streets and houses, pubs and churches, shops and public buildings have been placed where they are in relation to each other by men in the past, and for better or worse we still have to live with their decisions. When we wish to change the pattern even slightly we are

8

constrained by living history and have to take account of it. Even more powerfully are we influenced by the community itself, the intimate web of personal relationships we thread our way through every day, and this too is a product of history and understandable only in its terms. It is because of the nearness and intimacy of the local community and its physical environment that local history has become so popular in schools and evening classes throughout the country. Unfortunately, the universities have not kept up with this admirable trend, at least in their undergraduate courses, although it is probable that most postgraduate research is now done on local subjects. The main reason is that there is so much general ground to be covered in historical courses, and local history, though fascinating to do in depth, takes a great deal of time to do properly from the local sources. Except at a few universities like Leeds and Lancaster, therefore, it is postponed to the postgraduate level. In view of its fascination, usefulness and the keen demand for it in schools and adult education it is time, perhaps, that local history, in the sense used in Chapter 8 by Dr Marshall of the social, economic and political history of the local community, was taught as a matter of course to the potential teachers of history.

Having placed ourselves historically in our local and national environments, it is necessary to set ourselves in the wider context of what, following Toynbee, we may call our 'ecumenical' environment. Britain is a part of Europe, and Europe is the child of the Classical civilization of Greece and Rome. Our language, our literature, our art and architecture, our laws, our philosophic and scientific ideas, owe so much to the Classical world that ancient history is to all intents and purposes part of our own. It can be studied as part of a history degree at almost all British universities, though some of the newer ones have not yet provided for it, but in recent years it has mostly ceased to be a compulsory part. Its interest and attractions are discussed by Mr Creed in Chapter 3. In medieval times Europe was so much an integral entity, with a common language of scholarship and administration, a single Church and one

9

B

dominant political Empire, that the history of these islands cannot be separated from it, and they are dealt with together by Dr Tuck in Chapter 4. The break-up of this unity in early modern times is also best dealt with together, as it is by Professor Woolrych in Chapter 5. In modern times, too, European history has increasingly impinged upon our own, but is still generally studied separately, and is dealt with by a French specialist, Dr Church, in Chapter 9.

Until recently, most university degrees in history confined themselves to British and European history, except in so far as these impinged upon the rest of the world via wars and imperialism in courses on 'the expansion of Europe'. Now that the rest of the world is reacting so strongly against Europe, and that the centres of world power are shifting to Washington, Moscow and Peking, extra-European history is beginning to appear in many university syllabuses, at least in the form of optional courses. The first to appear in its own right and not merely as a phase in the history of the British Empire was the history of the United States, whose relevance to a world divided into pro- and anti-Americans is more than obvious, and the present role and status of American history is dealt with by Dr Heale in Chapter 10. Latin America has now surpassed the North as the continent of hope and fascination for many young people, but it is taught in relatively few history departments as distinct from Hispanic departments. The current situation in this thin but growingly important field is discussed by Mr Blinkhorn in Chapter 11.

Finally, the really dark continents for most Western historians are Africa and Asia, where two-thirds of the world's population live, but which attract least attention from our history departments and faculties. This is not because they are felt to be remote or less important, but because of the special difficulties of studying them at first hand. All the other continents are accessible to anyone with a reasonable command of the major European languages but, with the partial exception of India and South Africa, Asian and African history require a long apprenticeship to unfamiliar tongues, few Westerners ever attain to mastery of more than one or two of them, and when they do there is the further problem of getting to the archives and studying them on the spot. That is why the study of their history is concentrated in the School of Oriental and African Studies in London and a dozen other specialist departments elsewhere. But some of the specialists themselves would prefer to teach in general history departments, in closer touch with historians of other areas, and they are strongly in favour of those few history departments which offer African and/or Asian history as an option, to give at least some students a taste for them and supply them with postgraduates. Their interest and possibilities are discussed by Dr MacKenzie in Chapter 12.

Even where the whole range of historical studies described above is offered, there are still large areas of the history of mankind which are generally ignored. Pre-history has been omitted here in spite of its great interest, since it is normally studied in specialist departments of archaeology. The ancient and medieval history of most of the non-European civilizations are also generally left to specialist degree courses. British universities, unlike American, do not set out to teach 'world history' in the sense of marathon outline courses from the descent of man to his ascent into space. Even the chief British protagonist of 'universal history', Professor Geoffrey Barraclough, considers aggregate history of this kind to be, in Lord Acton's phrase, 'a rope of sand', and merely asks that we should concentrate in each age on the great events, men and peoples in a world perspective—and no existing history department, as far as I am aware, has followed even this admirable advice.

Yet in a sense this does not matter. History at the university is not an attempt to learn everything about everything. It is not *what* is studied but *how* it is studied that matters. Contrary to popular opinion, it is not a factual subject, an exhaustive narrative of events, the record of 'one damned thing after another'. It is an analytical subject, an attempt to discover the *significant* things that have happened, and *why* they happened, what *caused* them and what *they* caused in their turn. Historical research is like crime detection: it addresses itself to solving problems, to finding out not merely the critical ordering of the relevant facts but their meaning and interconnection, the aims and motives of the protagonists, the constraints and pressures of the surrounding circumstances, the place of accident and coincidence, the part played by human charity or malice, skill or clumsiness, success or failure. Like detection, it does this by taking one problem at a time and studying it in depth: the microscope is more informative than the telescope, a prowl round the garden more relevant than a world cruise. Like detection, too, it is a kind of multi-factorial analysis: it cannot afford to ignore any factor, any kind of clue, whatever level of experience it comes from, whether it is labelled political, social, economic, religious, moral, intellectual, technological, scientific, medical, psychological, or just plain human, frivolous or whimsical. Dealing as it does with the whole life of man in past society, nothing human is alien to it, and nothing human escapes its net. Like no other subject it gives an insight into human behaviour in all its manifold aspects. For where else than in the collective experience of men in past society will a knowledge of the infinite possibilities of human conduct be found?

And this is what makes it of use not merely to the layman and the citizen and to the professionals who teach them, but to everyone who has to deal with human beings in complex situations. Business and government of all kinds require, in addition to specialist knowledge, a general capacity to deal with complex human situations, to solve problems, to ferret out the relevant facts and perceive their significance and interconnection, to balance many incompatible factors, financial, legal, technological, psychological and just plain human, against each other, and arrive at some sort of conclusion about them. Now this is what historians do all the time. Even the traditional weekly essay at the university is nothing more than an attempt to assemble the significant facts about a particular problem and arrive at some sort of conclusion, under the critical eye of a tutor. And how much of management and administration consists of just this, the rapid appraisal of the relevant facts and factors of a problem, and the writing of a memorandum or report for the critical eye of the chairman or the minister! It is not so surprising, then, as an *Observer* survey found a few years ago, that the highest-paid graduates in industry by their middle thirties are historians. Who else can get, outside industry itself, the necessary breadth of vision and general training?

The final and most important use of history, though, is neither professional nor utilitarian. It is the sheer enjoyment of the subject, and the wealth of meaning it gives to life in whatever career one pursues. For what historians sell is understanding, understanding of the world around us and the people in it, in all their variety and colour. I for one am profoundly grateful that I am paid for doing what is, after all, one of the noblest, most permanent and fascinating activities of man.

SUGGESTED READING

BLOCH, MARC, *The Historian's Craft* (Manchester University Press, 1954).

KITSON CLARK, G., *The Critical Historian* (Heinemann, 1967).

COMMAGER, HENRY STEELE, *The Nature and the Study of History* (Merill: Prentice Hall, 1965).

ELTON, G. R., *The Practice of History* (Sydney University Press, 1967).

FINBERG, H. P. R. (ed.), *Approaches to History: a Symposium* (Routledge and Kegan Paul, 1962, paperback 1965).

GEYL, PETER, *Use and Abuse of History* (Yale University Press, 1955).

HALE, J. R. (ed.), *The Evolution of British Historiography* (Macmillan, 1967).

THOMSON, DAVID, *The Aims of History* (Thames and Hudson paperback, 1969).

WALSH, W. H., *An Introduction to Philosophy of History* (Hutchinson, 1958).

2

Finding out about History

Michael Argles

History is not just a parade of bare facts: it should train the mind and the intellect—as Professor Elton says, 'The historian should regard his subject as capable of training and equipping reasoning intelligences and should use it for that purpose.' (G. R. Elton, *The Practice of History* (1969), pp. 160-1.) In other words, history is not a soft option, and it should be used to develop your capacity to come to balanced and civilized conclusions by studying the facts, by reading and considering conflicting versions and opinions on those facts, and by learning to recognize and to reject all forms of false logic, verbal jargon, and illiberal prejudice. For example, one can hardly study the Indian Mutiny without reading the great standard work by Kaye and Malleson and the contemporary accounts by eminent soldiers like Roberts and Havelock, but one must certainly retain a balance by considering Edward Thompson's *The Other Side of the Medal* and the opinions of Indian writers like S. N. Sen. History, like mankind itself, is rarely black and white, and it will be your pleasure and your duty, in studying it, to assemble the evidence and to come to your own reasonable conclusions. That is what history is about and that is what civilized intellectual life is about; and if you want further weighty argument for this I advise you to read John Stuart Mill's *On Liberty,* in which you will find what is still the finest and clearest statement of liberal thinking and intellectual honesty.

When you are assembling your evidence you will read books; and to get books you will use libraries.

Libraries come in all sizes; but it is likely that you will be using fairly large university, college, or public libraries. Now a big library is an extremely complicated thing: many university libraries, for instance, have a quarter of a million books, with two thousand serial (journal) titles being received regularly. Really extensive libraries, like those at Oxford and Cambridge or the enormous foundations in some American universities, number their stock in millions. Indeed it is estimated that most American university libraries double their stock every twenty years! Practically every item in a library is an *individual* item and has to be treated individually—imagine a supermarket where every packet of soap powder, every tin of cat food, was different from the next, and each had to be described, catalogued, and accounted for. That is why libraries are complicated to organize and, inevitably, complicated to use. However, complicated things have a habit of getting surprisingly simple once you know the ropes, and the tricks and the dodges. Going to the moon is complicated, but not to the astronauts who have learnt the basic techniques. I am not suggesting that entering your library is like a moonshot, but it does help if you know what you are doing! So it is well worth finding out.

Libraries are arranged on a rational basis, and the first thing to do is to study the plan of the building (normally displayed near the entrance) and to see where everything is. Very often there are separate floors allocated to the arts, the sciences, the technologies, etc., and there will usually be special rooms or areas for such material as maps, rare books, or microfilms. Once you have mastered the basic arrangement you should only have to refer to the plan to confirm where certain classes of books are kept, or to get to a part of the library where you have not been before. In any case there should be adequate guiding throughout the building, to direct you to various sections, though regrettably this is not always so. It will also help you if you obtain the printed guide to the library. This usually includes the

15

regulations, and it will pay you to take note of these. They are not normally restrictive for the sake of restriction, but only to ensure that everyone gets a fair share of the book-stock, and to preserve the communal collections for future students and scholars.

The key to a library is its catalogue. This is a much surer way of finding what you want than by looking at the shelves (though this too has its uses)—after all it is not un-common for at least ten per cent of a library's books to be out on loan. Most catalogues nowadays are on cards, one card for each work, but some older libraries have printed catalogues. There is always an author (or name) catalogue, and very often another one in which the same entries are arranged in order of subjects. The classification number (or shelf mark) on the card will direct you, with the help of your plan, to the place where the book is shelved. Most large libraries arrange their books in some sort of subject order, though this often has to be combined with a shelf mark. Unfortunately the 'classification' (as it is called) is a most complicated matter, in which individual opinion may play a part, and which is further vitiated by the fact that knowledge is always changing and coalescing and that re-lationships which were clear fifty years ago are now much more intricate. The most commonly used schemes are the Dewey and the Library of Congress classifications, though others, such as Bliss and Universal Decimal, are also found. *All* schemes are imperfect, at times apparently illogical, frequently out-of-date, and often downright maddening, and librarians are very conscious of this. However, they do enable libraries to arrange their books in some sort of useful order, and the search for a perfect classification, like the search for the philosopher's stone, seems doomed to failure.

About one thing you should be clear: you are unlikely to find *all* the books on history in any one section of the library. For instance, economic history may well be with economics, constitutional history with politics, and so on, while special subjects like the history of education or the development of technology will be with education and technology respectively. So you will have to expect to use many sections of the library and to treat the catalogue, both author and subject sections, as your friend and adviser in this matter.

Talking of friends and advisers brings me to the library staff. They are there to help you, but do remember that they have many other responsibilities, the Librarian and his senior staff for developing and organizing the collections, both for the present and for the future, and the junior staff for doing many other important jobs 'out front' and 'behind the scenes'. You will generally deal with the girl behind the counter or service desk. She will probably be very friendly and obliging; but do remember that if she appears to you to be over-officious she is only doing her job according to the regulations and practices which have been drawn up for the benefit of the majority of users. And if she is pretty (which she often is), don't engage her in light conversation while a queue builds up behind you.

Librarians, by the way, are neutral, apolitical animals. To them Trotsky is as good as Lenin, Hinduism as Christianity. Their only constraint is how much money they have to spend on books—and, in universities and colleges, how the books they buy will fit in with the academic and teaching programme. Sometimes they get bad books; sometimes immoral books; sometimes politically undesirable books. One thing they never do is to refuse to buy a book solely on moral, social, or political grounds. Once a country refuses to have books like *Black Beauty* generally available (as South Africa, ludicrously, once did) or *Dr Zhivago* (as the Soviet Union does), so that country has become less civilized.

'Another damned, thick, square book! Always scribble, scribble, scribble! Eh! Mr Gibbon?' What the Duke of Gloucester would have said about today's output of historical works, one shudders to think. In 1968 about 1500 historical books were published in the United Kingdom alone. A typical university library takes at least one hundred historical journals; but the number of such journals published all over the world is fifty times as many—about five thousand. A basic historical source, such as the *Parliamentary Sessional Papers* for the nineteenth century, is contained on 46,000 microcards and costs £3,750. Historical literature is legion —but how to find out which parts of it you should read?

There are various ways of writing history, ranging from the racy and the vivid to the merely boring. The cardinal sins are pretentiousness and portentousness, either of language or of content, and the dishonesty of pretending to scholarship while in fact writing a book apparently based on no discoverable sources (or on sources which are not acknowledged). In fact, when assessing the worth of a book it is generally illuminating to turn to the footnotes or to the bibliography at the back. If references to other works are scanty or non-existent it is a fairly safe bet that the work is unscholarly or plagiaristic. On the other hand, 'popular' history should not be despised. Notable examples of it are the books of Arthur Bryant or Churchill's *History of the English Speaking Peoples*.

Winston Churchill provides us with a brilliant example of the first kind of history—the racy and the vivid, but founded on a decent amount of scholarship. Here is a passage from his *Marlborough,* which brings graphically to life the splendours and miseries of a sea-battle in the seventeenth century:

Grievous and cruel was the long struggle which ensued. The Suffolk shores were crowded with frantic spectators, the cannonade was heard two hundred miles away. From noon till dusk the battle raged at close quarters. The Dutch desperately staked their superiority with cannon and fire-ships against the English, tethered upon a lee shore. The Duke of York's flagship, the *Prince,* was the central target of the attack. Upon her decks stood the 1st Company of the Guards—Captain Daniels, Lieutenant Picks, and Ensign Churchill. Smitten by the batteries of several Dutchmen, assailed by two successive fire-ship attacks, and swept by musketry, she was so wrecked in hull and rigging that by eleven o'clock she could no longer serve as a flagship.
(Winston S. Churchill, *Marlborough,* Harrap, 1933, Vol. I, p. 82)

Consider also the opening paragraphs of G. M. Trevelyan's *Garibaldi* trilogy (an evocative description of Rome), and indeed the marvellous atmosphere created throughout this work, founded though it is on profound original research both in English and Italian archives. But for a plainly boring and tiresome recital, read James Tait's *The Medieval English Borough,* a book of immense scholarship by a very fine and dedicated historian, but lacking that vital spark and panache that marks the work of a really great and imaginative man. The fact is that a great historian must have scholarship, sympathy, and imaginative power—he must be able to bring a past age to life, while remaining meticulous in his learning. Such a man is Professor David Knowles, as a short and felicitous passage from one of his books will show:

The old prior was not a *littérateur,* nor was he, we may guess, one who received or gave affection readily or who passed through the darkness and light of a spiritual progress. It was given to him to rule Christ Church for a longer span than any other prior between the Conquest and the Dissolution; a young man when Albert the Great, Thomas Aquinas and Bonaventure were in their prime, he lived into the age of Ockham and Marsilio; he saw the papacy attain its highest flight, and lived on to the days of Avignon. While he developed his estates and organized his finances, Dante, in a world of intenser passions, found time to watch the fireflies in the vineyards of Fiesole and mark the dewdrops on the hillside grass in the starlit dawn, while Giotto was rendering imperishable the daisies and pencilled elms of Umbria. To Eastry, the primroses of the Kentish brookland, the harebells and ragwort of the downs, the whispering reeds and dazzling levels of Thanet were familiar sights, but of such things he does not speak, and perhaps did not think. He saw the pastures with the eyes of Shallow, not with those of Perdita; his thoughts worked the round of market prices, of stones of cheese, of bushels per acre, of the income from agistry, of the quality of the season's clip of wool. Stiff, dry and

19

masterful, a great high farmer and superbly able man of business, he passes before us as he rides about the manors or sits at the chequer. He died, still active, while celebrating Mass, in April 1331.

(David Knowles, *The Religious Orders in England*, C.U.P., 1948, Vol. I, p. 48 [Henry of Eastry]. Quoted by kind permission of Professor Knowles and the publishers.)

Historical novels are not to be despised, and one can still learn something about Erasmus from *The Cloister and the Hearth* by Charles Reade, or about the Pilgrimage of Grace from H. M. Prescott's *The Man on a Donkey*. If you are making a study of Edwardian England you can hardly fail to read *Kipps* and *The New Machiavelli* by H. G. Wells. However, don't overdo this, and get lured away by the 'Forsooth, knave' and 'La, Sir Percy' style of historical fiction or by the never-never lands of Sir Walter Scott.

So much then for the writing of history. If you want to read an entertaining and wise account of how and how not to write history, go to G. R. Elton's chapter on 'Writing' in his *The Practice of History*. (Elton, *op. cit.*, chap. iii.) Nor would a reading (or re-reading) of Sir Ernest Gowers' *Plain Words* come amiss. Short accounts of some of your models, famous historians, have appeared as parts of three useful series: *Writers and Their Work* (British Council/Longmans); the Historical Association's *General Series;* and the *Proceedings of the British Academy*.

When you get to university to read history, where do you get your books and what sort of books do you read?

To obtain your books you can either buy them, or borrow them from a library. A Government or L.E.A. grant to a student always contains an amount for books, and university libraries normally assume, when planning their stock, that students will use this money to buy essential texts recommended by their supervisors or tutors. Other useful purchases would be a good dictionary (e.g. the *Oxford Concise*), Fowler's *Modern English Usage,* Roget's *Thesaurus,* a reference book of historical dates, and a historical atlas.

However, you may like to add other favourite books of your own, and many of these are now likely to be available in paperback. Most universities have their own bookshops and the older university cities usually have at least one other good bookshop in which you can browse.

In vacations you will probably use your local public library and this may be able to obtain for you, through the national interlending scheme, any book not in its stock. In term, your university library will cater for your needs, either by lending or reference.

Books for the historian conveniently fall into three categories. They are: (1) Books on how and where to find out —these are usually known as 'bibliographies', and they range from simple introductions, through comprehensive booklists, to specialist guides to particular fields; (2) Reference books—encyclopaedias, dictionaries, and the like; (3) Texts—which may either be contemporary (e.g. Sergeant Bourgogne's account of the Retreat from Moscow) or subsequent (e.g. David Chandler's *The Campaigns of Napoleon*).

When you are an undergraduate most of your books will be texts, included in reading lists or recommended or suggested by tutors and lecturers. However, your reading should not be confined to these, and one mark of the university student is an ability to read widely and wisely and to have the facility, probably already developed in the sixth form, of 'gutting' a book or a chapter and extracting the essential information or message.

You should get used to using the library catalogue, and particularly its classified section and its attendant subject index. For lists of recent books consult the history sections of *British National Bibliography,* which lists every book published in the United Kingdom during the year. There are very many bibliographies and guides to historical literature and most of these are mentioned in a useful book by Philip Hepworth, *How to Find Out in History* (1966). This, though more likely to appeal to the postgraduate student, is a useful and extensive summary of sources. Its main drawback is lack of a good index.

Various attempts have been made to assemble lists of all books on history. The most successful is the American Historical Association's *Guide to Historical Literature,* very long (962 pages) and very detailed, and containing many annotations for the thousands of works listed. A standard guide to a more limited period is Ulysse Chevalier's frighteningly learned and all-embracing *Répertoire des Sources Historiques du Moyen Age,* while a slightly more approachable list for the same period is L. J. Paetow's *Guide to the Study of Medieval History.* Reviews of the literature issued during a particular period include the Institute of Historical Research's *Bibliography of Historical Writings Issued in the U.K., 1940-1945,* and its continuations up to the present day. The Historical Association's *Annual Bulletin of Historical Literature* is a well-informed narrative which describes and evaluates. Précis of articles in journals appear in *Historical Abstracts.* You can study recent and contemporary history by means of *Keesing's Contemporary Archives,* which describes national and world events from week to week in a loose-leaf form.

Examples of smaller lists and guides are:

John Roach (ed.), *A Bibliography of Modern History* (C.U.P., 1968). Intended as a bibliographical supplement to the *New Cambridge Modern History.* 'Primarily of use to schools and for undergraduate teaching' (Introduction), but wider in scope than this.

W. H. Burston and C. W. Green, *Handbook for History Teachers* (Methuen, 1962). Issued by the University of London Institute of Education. Contains 300 pages of annotated booklists.

Historical Association, *Modern European History, 1789–1945* (1960). *British History Since 1926* (1960). Two select bibliographies in the useful *Helps for Students of History* series.

Dillon's University Bookshop, *British Local History* (n.d.). A praiseworthy bibliography by a famous bookseller.

Invaluable guides to special techniques are:

Guide to the Contents of the Public Record Office (2 vols., 1963).

Amateur Historian, *The Historian's Guide to Ordnance Survey Maps* (1964).

A. M. Milne, *A Centenary Guide to the Publications of the Royal Historical Society, 1868–1968* (1968). This includes the important Camden Society series.

A. M. Milne, *Texts and Calendars, 1958*. A guide to important historical series.

G. Kitson Clark, *Guide for Research Students Working on Historical Subjects* (C.U.P., 1958). Commonsense and down-to-earth.

J. A. La Nauze, *Presentation of Historical Theses: Notes for University Students* (Melbourne U.P., 1966).

F. G. Emmison, *Archives and Local History* (Methuen, 1966).

Finally, two works which you will find fascinating if you like picking up unconsidered trifles:

F. M. Powicke and E. B. Fryde, *Handbook of British Chronology* (2nd ed., R.H.S., 1961). Will tell you countless facts about, for instance, English offices of state and their holders. Many valuable preambles and much bibliographical information.

C. R. Cheney, *Handbook of Dates for Students of English History* (R.H.S., 1945.) Deals with the vexed questions of dating, differing calendars, etc.

A good lead-in to a subject is to take a recent standard work on it and to look at references or booklists at the end of each chapter or of the book. This almost always has a snowball effect, a study of works listed leading to further references and so on.

Very often a judicious use of standard reference books will save you much time and trouble. *Encyclopaedia Britannica* is full of good, meaty stuff. It is important to remember that there is an invaluable index and that the latest (American) edition is not necessarily the most scholarly—the 11th edition of 1910-11 is still the finest for many purposes. Chambers' Encyclopaedia is shorter (about one-third the length) but it is authoritative and up-to-date and it is British in emphasis. If you read German or French, *Brockhaus* and *Larousse* are excellent, and most other countries have their own encyclopedias. The *Dictionary of National Biography* (21 volumes, with supplements) contains accounts of the famous, infamous, and not-so-famous. Its articles are often by the foremost authorities or by contemporaries of the subjects and there is nearly always a list of further references at the end of each entry. A similar, but international, work is Michaud's *Biographie Universelle,* and a potted version is *Chambers' Biographical Dictionary*. As far as Britain is concerned, *Who Was Who* and *Who's Who* bring

23

the story up to date. Specialist works like the *Oxford Classical Dictionary,* Hastings' *Encyclopaedia of Religion and Ethics* and the *McGraw-Hill Encyclopedia of World Art* are very often useful to historians.

Textbooks may be contemporary accounts or later evaluations. So far as undergraduate courses go the former are likely to be set books for various sections of the university course. They may be official or semi-official documents, such as those collected by the Public Record Office in London or by the Historical Manuscripts Commission; or they may be genuine on-the-spot descriptions or reminiscences 'recollected in tranquillity'. All should be used with a certain amount of care, because they may possibly be unreliable or biased—but who can know what it was really like to be an agitator in the early days of the Industrial Revolution unless he has at least read Samuel Bamford's *Passages in the Life of a Radical?* Contemporary accounts form one of the most exciting parts of the historian's raw material, and, of course, if you later go on to do post-graduate research in history you may enter the world of untouched documents, letters and records, or of medieval cartularies and classical archaeology, and this sort of detective work can be most stirring—if you doubt this read John Chadwick's account of the discovery of the key to the lost Cretan script by Michael Ventris (John Chadwick, *The Decipherment of Linear B,* 1960).

What other books will you be reading if you come up to university to study history? They will probably be mostly those written well after the events they describe. You should ask yourself six basic questions about any of these books.

(1) What are the author's qualifications for writing it?

(2) Has he allowed his social, political, and religious prejudices to influence him? (If so, you must make allowance for this in your assessment of his credibility.)

(3) What is the aim and scope of the book?

(4) Has it got a proper list of works to which the author has referred?

(5) Has it a competent index?

(6) What did knowledgeable reviewers say about it?

24

(But beware of personal spite—some academics are notoriously catty.)

You will want a passing knowledge of the great masters. Thucydides on Greek history, Bede on the early English, Clarendon on the Puritan revolution, should at least be familiar names. Gibbon is still immensely readable (though you will have to take some account of his boisterous anticlericalism). Macaulay and J. R. Green are often admired (though probably rarely read). Vinogradoff, Pirenne, Tout, Firth, Haskins, Mahon and Coulton are seven historians of the first rank. Trevelyan and Fisher, though nowadays perhaps in some sort of eclipse, followed the liberal tradition of urbane scholarship. Tawney and Namier ploughed new fields, of radical post-Marxian revaluation and exact political analysis respectively. The younger historians of today are carrying on this great heritage.

Fairly often historians have made attempts, sometimes successful, sometimes near-disastrous, to produce comprehensive works. J. R. Green in his *History of the English People* and A. J. Toynbee in *A Study of History* tried to do it alone; but usually it is a comprehensive effort of many hands. Such works are the *Cambridge Modern History* (13 volumes, 1902-26), the legacy of Lord Acton, a legendary Regius Professor at Cambridge; the *New Cambridge Modern History* (14 volumes, 1957-), some volumes of which have had a mixed reception; and the *Cambridge Medieval History* and *Ancient History,* both under revision. *The Oxford History of England* is a standard series, some volumes of which are quite outstanding; two foreign examples are the *Peuples et Civilisations* series and Meyer's *Geschichte des Altertums*. The (cultural) *History of Mankind* now being published by Unesco has creditable aims but suffers from the usual difficulties inherent in the assembling and editorial control of an international cadre of writers.

There has never been a time when more history books are being written than today. One only has to instance such specialist works as Steven Runciman's trilogy on *The Crusades,* E. H. Carr's history of the Russian revolution, or David Knowles's books on the monastic and religious orders,

25

c

to realize that the great tradition of historical scholarship is not dead. These books (and thousands of others) are yours for the asking if you come to university to study history. They may be entertaining and descriptive, or scholarly and contemplative, or (preferably) a combination of both.

One thing is certain: historians do not have to be obscure and lifeless in order to be scholarly. And there is no need for the jargon which painfully disfigures so many books nowadays, more especially those works of historical sociology which often (but not solely) come from the United States. Long words and pretentious sentences are no substitutes for tight thinking. Try, oh try, to distinguish technical terms (permissible in the right circumstances) from jargon, which is often used, as Geoffrey Elton says, 'as substitute for an explanation'. (Elton, *op. cit.,* pp. 105 ff.) One of the things you will learn from the intellectual study of history is a healthy horror of that 'Newspeak' in which meetings become 'confrontations', consultation becomes 'a continuing dialogue', and bombs to kill millions of people become 'nuclear devices'.

The materials for your study are here, in the great libraries and record repositories of this and other countries. Find out what tools and materials there are and learn to use them, and you will get not only a degree but perhaps a lifetime's enjoyment and pleasure as well.

3

Ancient History

John Creed

What do we mean by ancient history? An easy but superficial answer is 'the history of human society and culture
before the beginning of the middle ages'. But quite apart
from the difficulty of determining when antiquity ends and
when the Middle Ages begin, it is not easy to see how these
terms can be usefully applied to peoples outside the European
and Mediterranean areas; and, although Sir Michael Grant
in his book *Ancient History* includes as part of his subject-
matter the early history of India and China, most of those
who profess to study ancient history, and most university
courses in the subject, confine their attention to the ancient
history of the Middle East and the Mediterranean. Even
within this area, the study of the civilizations of Egypt,
Babylonia, Assyria, and Persia (as also the study of the
history of the Jews) is often treated as a separate and more
specialized subject than the two deeply interpenetrating
cultures of Greece and Rome. For better or worse, and
certainly with some loss of accuracy, the study of ancient
history is generally taken to be the study of Greek and
Roman history, and it is in this somewhat inaccurate
sense that I shall discuss it.

Even so, the field is a wide one. It embraces the civilizations about which we have learned so much in the past
century which flourished in Crete and on the mainland of
Greece in the second millennium B.C.; the rise and expansion
of the Greek city-states from the ninth to the sixth century;
the heyday of the Greek city-states, especially Athens, in

the fifth and fourth centuries; the expansion of Greek in-fluence throughout the Middle East in the wake of Alex-ander's conquest of the Persian Empire; the rise of the Roman Republic to a position of supremacy first in Italy and then in the Mediterranean as a whole; the internal political up-heavals which transformed the Roman state in the first century B.C.; and then the long history of the vicissitudes of the Roman Empire—a history which in one sense only comes to an end with the capture of Constantinople by the Turks in 1453 A.D., although the concern of the ancient historian with the empire does not generally extend much later than the disintegration of its Western part in the fifth century A.D.

A more positive approach to the question 'What is ancient history?' is to ask 'What kinds of things are we studying when we study ancient history, and what kinds of things can we hope to find out?' There is, of course, no easy answer to this question; different people will think different ques-tions the most important. But the character and limitations of the source-material at our disposal inevitably have the effect of channelling enquiries and interest in certain direc-tions—although even here we must be careful; the same source-material can be approached from many different angles, and used to ask many different questions. A political speech will not only tell us what its author intended to tell his audience, but also much that he and his audience took for granted although it is vital information for us; a piece of Greek pottery may give us information about the com-merce of the state from which it comes; it may also by its decoration give us information about matters of social habit or religious attitude.

Let me first say something about the source-material for ancient history, material which can broadly be divided into two categories, archaeological and literary. Archaeological material consists of the actual material remains of antiquity, much of it recovered by excavation, and may consist of buildings or ruins of buildings, pottery, jewellery, weapons and implements of various kinds—almost anything that has survived in a recognizable form. The interpretation

of these remains demands, of course, a very definite expertise (an expertise, let me hasten to say, which I do not possess
myself); but scholars can pronounce with reasonable certainty on the date and provenance of many remains,
judging both by their own characteristics and by the position
in which they have been found. (Such interpretation is of
course much easier when the remains are inscribed in a
decipherable language, but I am here talking mainly of
remains which are not so inscribed.) The importance of
this material is obviously very great. Perhaps the most striking change in our view of the ancient world over the last
century has been the uncovering by Heinrich Schliemann,
Sir Arthur Evans, and their many distinguished successors
of the remains of the Cretan and Mycenaean civilizations
of the second millennium B.C.; while our understanding of
life in the Roman Empire is enormously enriched by the
remains of Ostia and Pompeii.

It is perhaps at this point worth noticing the kind of information and understanding that we are likely to obtain
from archaeological sources on their own. In the first place,
we shall obviously obtain far more information than can
generally be derived from literary sources about the actual
material quality of life in the period to which the remains
relate; we shall know what swords were used, what armour
was worn, how the walls were decorated, how people were
dressed, something of their implements and utensils. But
further than this, particularly where there are such things
as pictures and statues, we shall gain some idea of people's
social habits, occupations and amusements, some insight
into religious practice, and sometimes, with some effort of
the imagination, into the underlying beliefs. Yet, on the
whole, archaeological evidence will tell us less about beliefs
than about practices; nor shall we learn much from such
material on its own about particular events (except sometimes destructive ones); we shall learn even less about particular decisions and the problems that led up to them. In
the main, then, the kind of information that we derive from
archaeology is likely to be generalized, indicating general
habits and characteristics, and to be external, in that, while

inferences may on occasions be made from it as to thoughts, intentions and policies, it cannot of itself provide such information in the same direct way as can recorded utterances. The situation is of course very different where archaeological evidence can be used in conjunction with literary material; our understanding, for instance, of the campaigns of the Roman governor of Britain, Agricola, in the first century A.D. has been greatly increased by the excavation within the last twenty years of military forts in Scotland; but here the archaeological material supplemented a literary account, and it was a condition of this increase of understanding that both kinds of evidence should be available.

But what is the literary or documentary evidence for antiquity? In one sense it is immense and illuminating, in another scanty and misleading. It is the outstanding feature of our knowledge of Greek and Roman antiquity that we have at our disposal a mass of literature which, quite apart from its aesthetic merits, contains the reflections of many minds, some of great acuteness and originality, on many problems, not least on those involved in the shaping and running of human society. This literature has come down to us through the patient labours of medieval copyists, and our most authoritative source for its contents lies in the medieval manuscripts that have survived till our own day (except in those rare cases where a piece of papryus has survived from antiquity in the sands of Egypt). This mass of ancient literature does not just include the works of Greek and Roman historians, important though some of these are, but a whole range of works including political and forensic speeches, plays, epic and lyrical poems, and works of philosophical enquiry, all of which help us to understand what can only be grasped occasionally from archaeological sources, the way in which certain people thought about moral, social and political problems, their reactions to what happened to them, to their contemporaries, and to their ancestors, and something of the actual course of political events. Sir Michael Grant has rightly deplored (*Ancient History,* p. 11) the notion that ancient history should merely be regarded as supplying the background to the study of the great Greek and Latin classical works. But equally it would be foolish to deny the illumination which these works shed on Greek and Roman history; indeed for many of us (and this is a point to which I shall return later) much of the interest of Ancient History derives from this self-conscious element, this critical reflection on events and actions.

But I said also that in another sense the literary evidence is scanty and misleading. It is obviously scanty if we set the bulk of literature produced in the thousand years or so of Greek and Roman antiquity against that produced in Europe in the five-hundred odd years since the invention of printing. But quite apart from this, there is a tremendous unevenness in respect both of time and of place in the distribution of this documentary evidence. We have a wealth (comparatively speaking) of information about the political life of Athens in the fifth and fourth centuries B.C., and of the Roman Republic in the first century B.C.; we are reasonably well-informed, too, about the Roman Empire in the first and the fourth centuries A.D. But our knowledge about Greek city-states other than Athens (except possibly Sparta) at any period is scanty in the extreme; we have really only a very sketchy knowledge of events in the first part of the third century B.C. and in the second and third centuries A.D., and even in the periods we claim to be well informed about there are tremendous gaps in our knowledge. There is a more general and more important point. A great deal of our literary evidence comes from an articulate and unrepresentative élite, and can for this reason give us a seriously distorted impression of the attitude of the ordinary Greek or Roman. It would be dangerous to infer from the political debates to be found in Thucydides' history and the plays of Euripides that the great mass of the Athenian citizen-body was passionately interested in politics and its principles (although there is more ground for believing something like this about fifth century Athens than about most ancient communities); it would be even more dangerous to suppose that the cultivated scepticism of Cicero or Horace gave us an insight into the attitude of an Italian peasant or artisan.

There is, however, one class of evidence which does something to correct this distortion. There have survived from antiquity a great variety and volume of inscriptions in varying degrees of completeness and intelligibility, stones, that is, on which both private and public utterances have been recorded; in many cases these inscriptions will be funeral memorials for some relative, will contain prayers or dedications to the gods, or will give records of the careers of deceased officials; sometimes stones will be inscribed with curses or incantations; in such ways inscriptions can sometimes tell us more than literary works can of the hopes, fears and beliefs of the ordinary man and woman. Inscriptions also do much to fill another gap in our record of antiquity —the lack, as compared with more recent periods of history, of official documents and records. Many inscriptions record decisions of official bodies, or contain official financial accounts and thus give us some reliable insight into the politics of the relevant period; indeed the exploitation by scholars of this epigraphical material has led to some of the most important advances in our understanding of the ancient world over the last century. Comparable with this evidence in its importance is the great mass of Roman legislation recorded for posterity by successions of Roman jurists.

How reliable, it may be asked, is all this evidence? In the case of archaeological evidence, of course, the appropriate question is rather 'What can we infer from the evidence?', and in a sense this is the appropriate question to ask, too, about documentary evidence—but the question we most immediately want to answer about a document is 'Have we reason to believe that the statements that it makes are true?', so that the question of reliability is clearly a proper and crucial one to ask. Scholars have tended to divide documentary material into what is primary—by which is meant what is written down at a time roughly contemporary with what is being described or talked about—and what is secondary—by which is meant what is written by people at a later time than the events and described on the basis of some source available to them but no longer so to us. There are obviously good reasons for making this division and for regarding 'primary' evidence as more valuable than 'secondary'. These reasons are reinforced in the case of antiquity by the habits of many ancient historians. Although there were a number of distinguished Greek and Roman historians, and although the Greeks may justly claim to have been the first to engage in the critical study of history, there was never developed in antiquity the systematically critical scrutiny of evidence which characterizes the modern approach to the subject. Thucydides, indeed, set great store by the careful sifting of the accounts of events that eye-witnesses gave him, and even his slightly more credulous predecessor Herodotus had more critical insight than he has sometimes been credited with. But with the possible exception of Polybius none of Thucydides' successors matched or even approached his rigour; historical works came to be regarded as legitimate vehicles for rhetorical talent and literary invention, and accounts received from earlier writers were often merely accepted and embellished, without any attempt being made to test the validity of their assertions except where there was a clear conflict of opinion between different authorities. There is thus good ground for accepting this division as a basis for working, and for setting higher value on such primary sources as inscriptions, political speeches, and histories written at the time of the events they purport to record, on the ground that the writers of these documents were in a better position than later writers to know what really did happen.

But at the same time we must note that there is a certain arbitrariness in this distinction between primary and secondary material. Contemporaries, too—even though they be as gifted as Thucydides—can make mistakes or be the victims of prejudice; and, after all, some contemporaries, even though they knew the truth, may not have wished to tell it. This situation is well illustrated by the period of ancient history for which contemporary literary evidence is most plentiful, the history of the Roman Republic between 70

33

and 43 B.C. The evidence is so plentiful largely because of the survival of a large amount of Cicero's voluminous correspondence and the bulk of his public speeches. This Ciceronian material conveys to us the atmosphere of Roman politics of the time in a way that is not possible for any other period of antiquity; but the fact that so much of the material comes from one source—and that source an active and argumentative politician—must put us on our guard against supposing that we can really form an adequate picture of the Roman political scene of even this period.

I hope that I have said enough to show the unevenness and inadequacies of our source-material, and the difficulties which this imposes on our study of ancient history; in the light of this, let me return to the question I posed earlier, 'What kinds of things are we studying when we study ancient history, and what kinds of things can we hope to find out?' As I have said before, the answers to these questions are likely to differ from one student of the subject to another, and my own answers will inevitably to some extent reflect my own predilections; in particular my own answers will probably seem to many colleagues to do less than justice to the kinds of question that arise from archaeological material.

A major interest of ancient history seems to me to lie in the emergence, along with accounts of events and incidents in themselves of importance, of a wealth of reflection and speculation on what is happening, on why it is happening, and on what should be happening. This speculative tendency is something that is rightly associated with the growth of Greek philosophy; but the tendency is not confined either to those whom we generally label as philosophers, nor indeed to Greeks; we find it in poets and dramatists; even more interestingly, we find it in those who record and those who participate in the political events of their day. When Herodotus writes his account of the great Persian invasion of Greece in 480-479 B.C., he portrays it as exemplifying the way in which the gods enviously strike down those who have attained to positions of inordinate power; when Thucydides writes of the great war between Athens and

34

Sparta, his history is dominated by an awareness of the moral and political problems that seemed to him implicit in the events of the war. In the same way, at a later stage, Virgil in his *Aeneid* tries to give a moral interpretation of the growth of Rome's power, while Cicero, whatever the limitations of his political achievements, is anxious in his speeches and treatises to uphold certain political principles.

The Greeks were not, of course, the first to reflect on the human predicament; we have only to read the Hebrew prophets to see that. But the interest is heightened by the fact that we can at the same time gain some insight into the actual political life of certain periods of Greek and Roman history. Despite all that I have said about the inadequacies and unevennesses of our evidence for antiquity, there are certain periods for which our records give us quite a lot of detailed information. The detail may be uneven, and may often present us with a biased picture; but we do know quite a lot about the political crises of Athens and Rome, and about the institutions and workings of these states. It is this combination of political action with political and moral reflection which gives a peculiar interest and flavour to the history of Greece and Rome.

Both the political thought and the political action of antiquity are strongly influenced, not to say conditioned, by the nature of what the Greeks called the *polis*, the city-state. It was the city-state which in many ways determined both the successes and the limitations of the Greek and Roman achievement in antiquity, and we must remember that even when the Mediterranean area was brought under the unified control of Rome, the city-state remained the basic political unit.

To take the positive aspects of the city-states first, the very smallness of their territories and populations made possible a degree of participation scarcely attainable in more large-scale organizations; and even in cities which were not by ancient standards democratic there was generally some sort of provision for the whole citizen-body—or at least that part of it which bore arms for the state— to express its assent to or dissent from the proposals put before it by the governing body. But in many states, particularly those in which there was commercial development, things went much further; in the highly developed democracy of Athens, the greater part of public business was transacted either by the assembly of the whole citizen-body or by a constantly changing and highly representative section of the citizen-body acting as an administrative council. Within these states we can see political debate and conflict engaged in at one and the same time on highly personal lines (and Greek and Roman orators were rarely inhibited about making scurrilous attacks on their political opponents) and with an explicit awareness of alternative political principles. Here we see for the first time those debates between those who champion the rights of all men to equality and those who claim special privileges for an élite; here too we see the emergence of the concept of the law as something whose claims have to be vindicated irrespective of the power or will of any particular ruler or group of rulers. Politics in fact was something in which the Greek was expected to engage, and questions of ethics and morality were for him difficult to separate from the political context in which he lived; and again this situation could scarcely have obtained but for the smallness and closeness of his community. This was the situation which Aristotle reflected when he remarked that man was by nature a *political* animal, an animal belonging to a *polis* whose citizen-body should not number more than one hundred thousand persons.

But the negative aspect of the city-states is scarcely less instructive. Each *polis* was fiercely jealous of its independence, keenly resenting any attempt to limit it. And so, although they shared a common language and a common culture, and although they depended upon each other in many ways, the Greeks found it peculiarly difficult to engage in any political combination. The very factors which made for an intensity of internal political life militated against any permanent alignment of states with each other and led to the decline in importance of the Greek city-states from the middle of the fourth century B.C. onwards. We thus see in Greek history in particular a demonstration of

36

the difficulties encountered by states keenly aware of their own political identity in devising or accepting any common and effective inter-state authority.

Along with this reluctance to combine went a kind of political exclusiveness. The Greek states thought of citizenship as something which belonged to those who sprang from the city's territory, and generally from its native stock. Indeed at the very stage when Athens was at its most democratic, it was insisting that citizen rights should only belong to those who were of Athenian parentage on both sides. Despite this, there were important ways in which Greeks thought of themselves as sharing a common descent, a common language, common religious cults, and a common tradition. But this wider sense of community in its turn gave rise to a further exclusiveness, a feeling of innate superiority to those who were innocent of any knowledge of the Greek tongue and could only say 'barbar', those whom they termed barbarians. The various modifications of and encroachments on this attitude form another instructive study in ancient history.

When we talk of city-states, we tend to think of the term as peculiarly applicable—at least within the field of ancient history—to the Greeks. But in fact, of course, Rome grew up as a city-state, and remained one in many ways until a comparatively late stage in her history. Here as with the Greeks we find conflict and debate on policies and principles; here too we find a keen sense of involvement in the affairs of the state as a whole; here even more clearly than in Greece there is a strong sense of the overriding importance of the law, to whose precise formulation so much attention was given by some of Rome's acutest minds. Yet Rome took on responsibilities far greater and over a far wider area than had ever been assumed by a Greek state, and she was for this reason very much a city-state with a difference. One of the most interesting features of Roman history in the pre-Christian era is the spectacle of a city-state, with a city-state's institutions, trying to govern a Mediterranean empire, and encountering enormous problems in the process; in the first century B.C. in fact the city-state institutions had to be so far modified that cynics might say that they retained only a ceremonial existence. Yet it would be hard to imagine that Rome could ever have attracted the loyalty which she eventually commanded—and this is not to pretend that her rule was not often resented, and justly resented —but for her republican and city-state origins. But this expansion of the field of Roman loyalty was also aided by another factor. From quite an early stage, a situation arose in which Roman citizens were living some distance from Rome itself, and yet remained Roman citizens. In one way, this meant that the actual content of citizenship was diminished, since many citizens were unable, simply for reasons of distance, to participate in the political meetings at Rome. But it also made it possible to pursue a policy which is deeply embedded in the Roman tradition of being generous in the bestowal of Roman citizenship on persons who were not Roman by birth. This also helped to ensure that loyalty to Rome could reasonably be felt by people living far away from the city-state which had become the seat of government of an empire.

I have stressed the city-state as a feature of antiquity because it seems to me a very central feature; at the same time I think we can see that some of the problems confronting the city-state were not altogether dissimilar from our own: how do we ensure that people have a sense of participation in their political community? how can states engage in effective political combination without compromising their freedom? how far can a state go in assimilating aliens without losing its identity? But I would not wish to suggest that there are not other important and interesting features to attract our attention. It is easy to see in the relations between Athens and Sparta in the fifth century B.C. the tension of two states roughly equal in power and proclaiming opposed ideologies; the collapse of the Roman republic in the first century B.C. in the face of military adventurers highlights a perennial problem never entirely solved by the Romans—how to subordinate the army to the civil government. Again, the fact that the ancient world was the world into which Christianity was born gives particular interest to the religious habits and beliefs of the ancient world, their relation to the political order, and the relation between Christianity and the forces it encountered in the first four centuries of its development.

I have said something, I hope, to indicate that ancient history is interesting because in it we see man and society wrestling with problems which are in some cases inseparable from the human condition, in others seem to have a contemporary ring. I could add that the influence of both Greece and Rome on the development of modern Europe has been immense and that, in that way too, much may be learned about the background to our own times and culture. But at the same time it would be fatal to concentrate on those aspects of ancient history which appear to have a resemblance to the history of our own time or to suppose that the value of ancient history lies solely in its imagined topicality. If we are studying the working of Athenian democracy, it is of the highest importance to observe the profound differences of its social structure and social life from those of our own times; if we are studying the relation of Christianity to the other religions of the Roman Empire, it is important to realize how differently the nature of a religion was viewed by the ancients. Any understanding of antiquity will be seriously distorted which does not try to understand these differences.

But this need to understand differences does not diminish, rather it increases the value of the study of ancient history. If the ancient world really were almost the same as our own, there would be no particular point in studying it rather than our own. Indeed, a very important part of its value, as with all worth-while subjects of study, lies in the fact that it enlarges our imaginations by forcing us to look at something unfamiliar which should challenge our assumptions and force us to question much that we have taken for granted.

SUGGESTED READING

GRANT, Sir Michael, *Ancient History* (Home Study Library, Methuen, 1952).

HISTORY

BURN, A. R., *The Pelican History of Greece* (Penguin, 1966).

FORREST, W. G., *The Emergence of Greek Democracy* (World University Library, 1966).

WARDE FOWLER, W., revised M. P. Charlesworth, *Rome* (Home University Library, 1947).

SCULLARD, H. H., *From the Gracchi to Nero* (Methuen, University Paperbacks, 1959).

BALSDON, J. P. V. D., *Julius Caesar and Rome* ('Teach Yourself History', Hodder and Stoughton, 1967).

CHARLESWORTH, M. P., *The Roman Empire* (Home University Library, 1951).

JONES, A. H. M., *Constantine and the Conversion of Europe* ('Teach Yourself History', Hodder and Stoughton, 1948).

HERODOTUS, *The Histories* (*Tr*. A. de Selincourt, Penguin, 1954).

THUCYDIDES, *The Peloponnesian War* (*Tr*. R. Warner, Penguin, 1954).

WILKINSON, L. P., *Letters of Cicero* (Hutchinson University Library, 1966).

TACITUS, *The Annals of Imperial Rome* (*Tr*. M. Grant, Penguin, 1956).

4

Medieval History

Anthony Tuck

The study of medieval history is unfashionable. In the
first half of this century it was taken for granted as an
essential part, perhaps the pre-eminent part, of a university
degree in history, and medievalists felt no need to urge their
discipline's claim to a large share of an undergraduate's
time. But in the last two decades, medieval history has
lost its pre-eminent position. A recent survey (*History at
the Universities,* ed. G. Barlow, Historical Association, 1968),
has shown that, of the forty universities in the United
Kingdom which offer full courses in history, only twenty-
five require students to take a paper in medieval English
history; sixteen require a paper in medieval European history; and one university, Cambridge, requires its undergraduates to take one paper on a medieval subject. Furthermore, in most of the new universities medieval history oc-
cupies only a peripheral position. Only one of the eight
new universities requires its history students to take a
paper in exclusively medieval English history. Four of the
eight—Essex, Stirling, Warwick, and Ulster—offer no medieval history at all. Sussex offers no medieval English
history before 1349, and only certain periods of medieval
European history; while East Anglia and Kent provide no
medieval European history at all. Only York and Lancaster
have a sufficient range of courses to permit a substantial
degree of specialization in medieval history. At Lancaster, a
student is able if he wishes to take five out of his six History

41

major finals papers in medieval subjects, and a roughly similar degree of specialization is possible at York.

The decline of medieval history clearly requires explanation. Ideally, perhaps, the burden of explanation should lie upon those who assert that medieval history is *not* worthwhile; it should be for them to establish what standards entitle one to approve of history but to disapprove of medieval history. The existence of such a standard will be discussed shortly; but there are other, perhaps less important, reasons for the decline of medieval studies. Undoubtedly, one reason is the decay of Latin teaching in schools, especially in the sixth form. For although it is possible to pursue an outline course in medieval history with only a very rudimentary knowledge of Latin, it is neither possible nor desirable for students without at least O-level Latin to tackle semi-special or special subjects in medieval history; and such students are entering universities in increasing numbers. Changes in the school curriculum thus directly affect the well-being of medieval history in the university; and so too do changes in the university curriculum itself. The increasing popularity of combined or even multi-subject degrees necessarily leads to greater selectivity in historical periods covered, and the medieval period has sometimes been the first to be eliminated. But changes of this nature do not provide the whole explanation. There is perhaps a widespread but wholly unjustified prejudice against the middle ages: the very term *medieval* is a common journalistic term of abuse. One need look no further than the pages of *Lucky Jim* to see such a prejudice exemplified : 'Had people (Dixon thought) ever been as nasty, as self-indulgent, as dull, as miserable, as cocksure, as bad at art, as dismally ludicrous, or as wrong as they'd been in the Middle Age?' (Kingsley Amis, *Lucky Jim*, Penguin ed., 1961, p. 87). Medievalism has become vulgarly synonymous with irrational obscurantism. It is hard to tell how powerful or influential such a prejudice is amongst sixth-formers and undergraduates, but it may help to shape attitudes. More seriously, and more importantly, there has been a trend in recent years away from technical and specialized history. The analysis of a charter, the acquisition of detailed knowledge of the medieval legal or administrative system, has been held to be useless; and perhaps because medieval history is more concerned with technicalities than are other periods, it has suffered accordingly. But perhaps the most important reason for the decline of medieval history is the pressure for relevance and contemporaneity in university history courses. As long ago as 1945 Professor Beloff remarked that 'there is increasing pressure at every level of historical teaching for the syllabus to include more recent periods.' Professor Barraclough's campaign on behalf of contemporary history is well-known; and in the discussions on the reform of the Historical Tripos at Cambridge in 1966 it was held that an increase in the attention given to modern non-European history would have to be achieved partly at least at the expense of medievalism.[1] This pressure rests on assumptions which have been discussed and criticized in an earlier chapter; but it is perhaps the most serious threat to the university study of medieval history. The crudely utilitarian question, how would one justify the study of medieval history to the taxpayer, may underlie some of the discussion about the place of medieval studies in the university curriculum.

But in combating arguments for contemporaneity and relevance, medievalists join with historians of most other periods, and it is not the purpose here to argue the reasons for the study of history in general: such ground is most treacherous. The medievalist would argue that the middle ages is as much worth studying as any other area or period into which history is divided: the part stands or falls with the whole. From the point of view of undergraduate education, however, there are two points worth making about the study of medieval history in particular. First of all, there is much to be said for undergraduates spending some part of their time studying a period different from the ones they are used to, and especially different from our own time. The student who approaches the middle ages has to come to understand a civilization based on social, political, and even perhaps religious assumptions which will be unfamiliar to him. He will come to appreciate a different attitude to the state, and to political loyalties—seen, for much of the middle ages, in personal rather than abstract terms. In the intellectual world, he will find a greater unity of subject matter—especially of theology and philosophy—and a greater cohesion in the world of learning, held together by the Latin language and the international church. He will come to appreciate the economic basis of medieval society—overwhelmingly rural and agrarian, with the possibilities for economic growth severely restricted by the limited technical knowledge of the period. And he will have to deal with societies that are isolated, dependent upon slow and poor communications, and upon the oral transmission of ideas—circumstances which, as Marc Bloch has shown, have occasionally recurred in the modern world. (He compared 'the propagation of false rumours in the trenches in the first world war' with the spread of news in the 'isolated societies of the early middle ages'.)[2] But the middle ages is not only different and remote in time: it is also the direct ancestor of our own civilization, and there are thus certain familiar landmarks which provide a basic frame of reference. In England in particular, such landmarks abound. Many of our institutions—most notably parliament—originate in the middle ages; our legal system first began to take shape in the twelfth century; and the familiar pattern of county divisions is, in the southern two-thirds of England at least, an inheritance from the Anglo-Saxons. Furthermore, the existence of so many physical survivals from the middle ages—cathedrals, abbeys, parish churches, manor houses—acts as a stimulus to seek understanding of the periods when they were built, the purposes they served and the quality of life they sustained; they also provide a sense of direct contact with the middle ages. The confusion and perplexity aroused by total unfamiliarity are thus avoided. The second and more important point concerns the quality of the literature and the level of scholarly activity in the field. A subject is worth studying at university level only if it is maintained by a satisfactory body of literature and by the activity of distinguished scholars working in the field. In both these respects medieval history is well served. It has engaged the attention of outstanding historians in this country and abroad— Stubbs and Maitland in the late nineteenth or early twentieth centuries; more recently, Marc Bloch, Sir Frank Stenton and Dom David Knowles. The work of such men should be read by anyone having a historical education. And the present generation of scholars is actively reinterpreting the period, and engaging in controversies as lively as anything in the later period. Questions such as the nature of late Anglo-Saxon society, the origins of feudalism, the origins of parliament, and the effects of war and plague on late medieval French economy and society provide the basis for scholarly debate. And the discussion of the nature of Tudor government in England has been shaped partly at least by work being done on late medieval English government.

But though the arguments for the study of medieval history may be those for the study of history in general, the nature and sources of the subject dictate a more distinctive approach. The problems presented by the character and quality of the evidence, and by the interaction with other disciplines, are different from the problems faced by historians of more modern periods, and the character of medieval history can perhaps best be illuminated by discussing these problems.

First of all, it is essential to remember that the medieval period, customarily taken to be the thousand years between the fall of the western and the fall of the eastern Roman Empires, is hardly a uniform period. The study of the so-called dark ages, from the collapse of the western Roman Empire until about 1000, raises very different problems from the study of the civilization of the high middle ages; and the fourteenth and fifteenth centuries differ sharply from earlier centuries in political and economic structure and in intellectual outlook. Indeed, in England the close similarities between late medieval and early modern politics and administration have been emphasized in much recent work and recognized in some university syllabuses.

The most obvious difference between the history of the

dark ages and that of subsequent centuries lies in the nature
and quantity of the evidence. From about the twelfth century, western European rulers began to develop administrations which produced and retained systematic written
records of their activities; so too did individual landowners,
lay and ecclesiastical; and from thenceforth it becomes
possible to write detailed political, economic and administrative history from record sources. But for the earlier period
there is no such systematic body of material. There are
chronicle sources, narratives written, chiefly by ecclesiastics,
often decades and sometimes centuries after the events they
describe; and records, chiefly deeds and charters. But the
records are few in number, their survival determined by
chance rather than by bureaucratic routine, and the chronicles are neither as numerous nor as reliable as they are for
later centuries. It is almost impossible, therefore, to write
the history of this period entirely from written sources;
though for Anglo-Saxon history Bede and the Anglo-Saxon
Chronicle provide an indispensable foundation. Even the
written sources for this period, however, present serious
difficulties. Much of our scanty knowledge of the early
church in the British Isles, for instance, comes from saints'
lives which have to be controlled by other evidence before
they can be accepted as trustworthy. Similarly, the Norse
sagas provide much information about the settlement of
Iceland and Greenland; but they were often written down
two or three hundred years after the events they describe
took place, and their historicity, as Professor Gwyn Jones
points out, must be established by checking them 'with
every known source of information, where possible with the
archaeological record.' (G. Jones, *The Norse Atlantic Saga*,
1964, p. 37.) And recently archaeological work in Greenland has strikingly confirmed some of the detail in Eirik's
saga and The Greenlanders' saga. The problems of reliability and trustworthiness in such sources are easy to
identify, if hard to solve; but similar problems arise even
with so familiar and apparently historical a source as the
Anglo-Saxon Chronicle. The relationship between the various MSS of the Chronicle is difficult to establish, and the

46

sources of each version hard to identify. Further, much of the Chronicle was written from the west Saxon point of view—a bias to be borne in mind when using it—and it provides little information about events in the north during a crucial period of Scandinavian settlement there in the tenth century. But history, as Marc Bloch pointed out, is not merely a matter of documents. Other disciplines can contribute to the widening and deepening of our knowledge of the past, and to the early medievalist archaeology, philosophy, numismatics, and perhaps anthropology can provide new evidence and suggest new questions to ask. The co-ordination of archaeology and history has perhaps made possible the greatest advance in our understanding of the Dark Ages. Excavation in certain English cities has compelled a revision of the previously held views that few, if any, towns were continuously occupied from the third to the seventh centuries; the distribution of Saxon burials in Yorkshire tells us much about the Saxon take-over of that county, and suggests that Saxon rule originated in a revolt by mercenaries in York and then spread outwards rather than in an invasion from the east coast; and, to take a later example, excavation of Norman Castles on the south coast may overturn the belief that the Saxons knew little of the art of castle-building. But archaeological evidence has serious limitations. As Dr Wainwright pointed out, it provides 'direct evidence (only) of practical skills, technological processes, aesthetic interests and physical sequences. (F. T. Wainwright, *Archaeology and Place-Names and History* 1962 p. 9.) For it is concerned only with material remains, and can tell us little or nothing of such abstract matters as social structure, or political and legal systems. Second only to archaeology in its importance for dark age history is philology, in particular the study of place-names. For instance, linguistic analysis of place-names can throw light on the whole question of Scandinavian immigration into England. There is no record in the written sources of Scandinavian migration to north-west England in the tenth century. Yet there are very large numbers of place-names in that area which embody Scandinavian personal names and names of natural features. The names are Norwegian rather than Danish, suggesting that the Scandinavian settlement there was not an extension of Danish settlement in the East Midlands and Yorkshire. Furthermore, some of the names embody Irish grammatical constructions—Aspatria, Brigsteer—with the adjective after the noun. (Aspatria—Patrick's Ash; Brigsteer—Styr's Bridge.) Scholars have therefore concluded that the north west was settled by Norsemen who had earlier established themselves in Ireland but were driven out, perhaps after military defeat. No chronicle source mentions this migration: its discovery was essentially a consequence of place-name study. But neither archaeology nor philology, nor for that matter numismatics, throws much light on more abstract matters such as social, political, and legal systems: and any information they do provide is likely to be incidental, indirect, and fragmentary. In understanding these aspects of the dark ages, the historian is thrown back on the written sources, though it is by no means impossible that social anthropology may suggest questions and offer insight on such general problems as the relationship between lordship and kinship in dark age society. Anthropology, too, may help historians to understand more clearly the nature of belief and superstition not only in the dark ages but throughout the middle ages and beyond. For example, Claude Levi-Strauss's concept of a tension between belief and unbelief in primitive peoples' approach to magic and divination may suggest an approach to the problem of whether so intelligent and sophisticated a king as Richard II actually believed in the arts of astrology, geomancy, and physiognomy which so interested him.[3]

But even when other disciplines have been co-ordinated with history, there are bound still to be gaps in the evidence, bound always to be periods about which we know little from any source. And even though some of the most interesting developments in the history of this early period have come at the point where history connects with other disciplines, the historian cannot scrutinize the evidence produced by, say, an archaeologist with the same critical care that he can bring to the scrutiny of his own kind of evidence, documents. However, these considerations apply primarily to dark age and early medieval history. The later the period of medieval history one studies the better the documentary evidence is likely to be, and the easier it becomes to control chronicle narratives by reference to record sources. For in both England and in most of the states of western Europe, the twelfth and thirteenth centuries were marked by a great growth in the activities of governments and administrations, public and private, lay and ecclesiastical. Government became more a matter of written instruction and record, less a matter of oral direction and tradition; and governments—and private individuals—who produce and rely upon written record provide the historian with the major part of his raw material.

Yet although the difficulties of obtaining material perhaps diminish, problems of interpretation remain, and can best be illustrated by a discussion of a particular aspect of medieval history, the political history of medieval England. It has long been popularly assumed that medieval English political history is merely a matter of kings and things—of classifying English medieval rulers into good kings and bad kings, and, perhaps, in view of the effect a reign was held to have had on constitutional development, into good things and bad things: John was a bad king but a good thing, because as a result of his misgovernment Magna Carta was promulgated. The crudity of such an approach conceals an essential point, that medieval government, in both England and the countries of western Europe, was seen as essentially personal. In the early middle ages at least, a man's primary loyalty was to his feudal lord; his loyalty to his king too was expressed in personal terms, and a sense of loyalty to an abstract entity such as the state was very imperfectly developed. Even the idea of community, which developed in England early in the thirteenth century, was both a personal and a territorial concept. Furthermore, throughout the middle ages in England at least, the governing group consisted of a small group of lay and ecclesiastical nobles, all intimately known to one another, often closely related to one another, and frequently jealous of one another. And because political conflict is so often conflict within this small ruling group, personal factors carry great weight. Equally, because government was regarded as essentially a matter for the king, because the initiative in virtually all matters lay with him, his personality, his capacity for the job, matter greatly. His skill and tact in handling his nobility, his willingness to pay due regard to magnate pressure and prejudice in choosing his advisers and councillors were essential if political stability were to be maintained. Political strife, as Mr McFarlane has remarked of the civil wars of the mid-fifteenth century, might well arise principally because of the personal failings of the kings themselves.[4] The student of medieval political history, therefore, has to understand and interpret personality and appreciate the crucial role that differing personalities might play in provoking political change in a society whose basic political structure remained remarkably stable. Yet the interpretation of personality is a difficult exercise at all times, and particularly difficult when the evidence on which interpretation is based is mediated through sources whose standpoint is very different from our own. As Professor Galbraith pointed out,[5] medieval chroniclers understand only a limited range of personalities. They are most at home with men who correspond most precisely to certain standard medieval types—the saint, the warrior, the judge. Henry III, Edward I, and Edward III emerge with much more clarity from the medieval chronicles than do more complex figures such as Edward II or Richard II; and in interpreting the personalities of such men it is essential to bear in mind the limitations and prejudices of medieval writers. But part of the fascination of work on Richard II lies in a gradually growing understanding from the sources of a complex, intelligent, and unusual character.

However, the part played in medieval politics by personality should not be overemphasized. Medieval history is not simply kings and barons. Indeed, there may be some danger that the activities of central governments generally will be overemphasized. For in studying medieval government, one is not studying the deliberate implementation of legislative programmes, the management of an economy, or the inducing of social changes. Medieval governments were to a large degree unsophisticated economically and socially, and governments induced economic changes as a rule only accidentally, the unforeseen consequences of political or fiscal measures. Medieval governments were much more concerned with maintaining, extending, and reconciling rights: government was above all seen as a judicial act, even the fiscal process of the Exchequer assuming something of the character of a judicial hearing. The seal of the first Capetian king of France showed him, not mounted as a warrior as one might expect, but seated as a judge, and throughout the middle ages the judicial function of kingship was regarded as pre-eminent. Legislation, especially in England, frequently arose in response to the need to do justice in particular cases; the distinction between justice and legislation is often almost imperceptible, and the maintenance of law is an essential duty of kingship. As Dr Storey points out, in *The End of the House of Lancaster* (1966), p. 60, Henry VI's failure to maintain law and to do justice was a fundamentally important reason for the growth of support for the Yorkist faction in mid-fifteenth century England. Medieval governments, arguably, reacted more often than they initiated, and in order to understand their activity it is essential to analyse the local, sectional, and even personal pressures that brought government into action.

For these reasons, local history has perhaps a greater bearing on national history than has sometimes been realized. Local communities in England had a high degree of self-consciousness and a strong sense of cohesion. They were experienced in self-government, and ready and willing to make their wishes and their grievances known to king and ministers.[6] The vitality of local communities goes some way towards explaining the importance in parliament of their representatives, the members of the Commons. In France, of course, and in Germany and Italy also, local particularism became much stronger than in England. The

acts of the early Capetian kings of France have little significance outside their own lands, the Ile-de-France and the
Orléannais, and a wholly misleading impression of twelfth-
century French history is gained if the student concentrates
only on the kings and the sources which recount the activities of the kings, such as Abbot Suger's life of Louis VI.
Political developments in the great feudal principalities
proceeded at a similar pace to, perhaps even in advance
of, developments on the royal demesne, and the history of
both, the interaction between the two, must be studied if
early medieval France is to be satisfactorily understood.
Throughout the middle ages, the outlook of the French
nobility was local rather than national, and this outlook,
which differed so much from that of their English counterparts, goes far towards explaining the political and constitutional developments of later medieval France. In both
countries, too, political rivalries at the centre were often
little more than the continuation of feuds which were local
in origin, and intervention by central government in the
local liberties and influence of a noble might bring a violent
reaction at the centre: the struggle between York and
Lancaster in the mid-fifteenth century is a good example
of the escalation of local feuds; the support of Bolingbroke
by the Percies in 1399 a good example of a magnate inter-
vening in national politics primarily to protect his local
interests. In studying the interaction of personal, local,
national, and royal interests, in analysing the extent to
which the central government was willing and able to exert
its authority in the localities, lies much of the fascination
of medieval political history.

But just as medieval society was in some ways much more
localized in interest and outlook than our own, so too it
was in other ways more international. Many political theorists assumed the existence of a universal Christian empire
in which Pope and Emperor were equal and co-ordinate
powers and in which the territorial units of the west were
subsumed. But such a concept was in practice quite meaningless. And the more limited idea of a Holy Roman Empire
extending over most of what is now Germany, Austria,

Bohemia, the Low Countries and Northern Italy was little more than a political myth. Indeed, as Professor Barraclough has argued,[7] the less real it was the more elaborate became the myth. The internationalism of the middle ages—perhaps better called the non-nationalism—is not the same thing as the universalism of political theorists. But though there was no universal Christian Empire, nor was there a rigid state system of the kind that developed in more modern periods. In continental Europe at least, different political authorities overlapped and interlocked with great complexity, and it was never easy to say where the frontier of any particular kingdom, county or duchy ran. Men were clear that a kingdom was an entity different in kind, perhaps more enduring, than a county or duchy: it is significant that the only feudal principality which became a kingdom in the middle ages was Portugal: and from the mid-thirteenth century onwards men began to recognize some loyalty to the entity they called, under the influence of the revived concepts of Roman law, their *patria*. But relationships between states were still more concerned with the definition and enforcing of particular rights inherited or claimed by the ruler than with increasing national territory or prestige. The concept of the nation was still imperfectly developed. The overlapping and interlocking of different rights, and the dissension to which such complexity gave rise, is nowhere better illustrated than in the history of England and France in the period from 1066 to 1214, when John finally abandoned his attempt to hold on to Normandy, or perhaps even until 1453, when the English were finally evicted from Gascony. From the political standpoint, in the period from 1066 to 1214, England was hardly an entity in herself, but merely a part, and 'not always the most important part',[8] of a wider unit, the feudal inheritance of the House of Anjou. The Angevin kings of England were French in origin; their inheritance covered much of western France, as well as England, and England claimed only a share of the attention of her kings. Henry II was much more French than English. He was born at Chinon, he died at Colombières and is buried at Fontevrault; and he spent appreciably less than half his reign in England. It was his inheritance, not the English nation in particular, which he defended against the kings of France, and the reasons for conflict are to be found more often in the French than in the English dominions of the House of Anjou. As T. F. Tout justly remarked, 'English and French medieval history are one subject.'[9]

But in ecclesiastical and intellectual matters, the non-nationalism of the middle ages is even more apparent than in its politics. From the mid-eleventh century onwards, the popes developed a legal and administrative system which imposed uniformity, under papal leadership, on the western church, and the popes developed a theory of supremacy in western Christian society which was of practical significance mainly in their conflicts with the rulers of Germany but which gave renewed vitality to the idea of universal authority in church and state, an idea which was only gradually undermined in the course of the fourteenth century. As the papacy developed into an international organization, so the clergy in the countries of western Europe found that they had double loyalties—to king and pope—and the rulers found that they no longer enjoyed unquestioned authority over their clergy. In these conflicts of interest between local rulers and the international church lies much of the interest of medieval ecclesiastical history.

The church, however, was more than a political, diplomatic, and administrative organization. It was also responsible for most of the education which medieval men received, and its members played an overwhelmingly important part in the intellectual and cultural life of the period, in monasteries, cathedral schools, and, from the mid-twelfth century onwards, in the universities. There was mobility amongst individuals—Anselm, for instance, was born in 1033 in Aosta, within the dominions of the kingdom of Burgundy; he was educated at the monastery of Bec in Normandy, and ended his career as Archbishop of Canterbury. And the mobility of men led to the mobility of ideas: philosophical and theological ideas, political and social theories, fashions in religious life, art, and architecture,

enjoyed an international circulation, though the latter
were often subtly modified in different parts of Europe.
This international culture was held together by the use of
Latin : indeed, in *De Vulgari Eloquentia* Dante argued
that Latin was a conventional literary language maintained
so that men of differing vernacular speech might understand one another.[10] He did not seem to appreciate that the
vernaculars of France, Spain, and Italy were developments
from Latin.

The civilization which I have attempted to describe developed in western Europe from the late eleventh century.
But in the east a very different civilization developed,
shaped by its Greek basis, its Roman inheritance, and by
its relationship with Islam, the Slavonic peoples, and, after
the first crusade was launched, with the westerners. Though
medieval western civilization was, within itself, international,
it was intensely local when seen in a wider perspective.
The history of medieval Byzantium, of medieval Islam, and
of the Slavonic lands of north-eastern Europe is important and interesting, but beyond the scope of this essay. The
student of the medieval west, however, should not forget
that though medieval western civilization is to a great extent
intelligible on its own terms, it developed in only a part
of the lands ruled by the Romans to whom the medieval
west was so much indebted. The amount of attention
given to Britain and Western Europe in this discussion
perhaps reflects the extent to which they dominate university
syllabuses and the horizons of scholars: but for a complete
understanding of medieval Europe, knowledge of the Greek
east is as important as knowledge of the Latin west.

SUGGESTED READING

BLOCH, M., *Feudal Society* (1939; English translation, Routledge and
    Kegan Paul, 1961).
DAVIES, R. R., 'Marc Bloch', *History*, LII, 1967.
GALBRAITH, V. H., *The Public Records* (O.U.P., 1934).
GALBRAITH, V. H., 'Good Kings and Bad Kings in English Medieval
    History', *History*, xxx, 1945.
HAY, D., *The Medieval Centuries* (Methuen, 1964).

SOUTHERN, R. W., *The Making of the Middle Ages* (Hutchinson, 1953).
WAINWRIGHT, F. T., *Archaeology and Place-Names and History* (Routledge and Kegan Paul, 1962).
WOLFF, P., *The Awakening of Europe* (Penguin, 1968; *The Pelican History of European Thought,* vol. 1).

CHAPTER NOTES

1. M. Beloff, 'The Study of Contemporary History: some further reflections', *History*, xxx, 1945, pp. 75–84; *Cambridge University Reporter*, 2nd February 1966, pp. 1013–27, esp. pp. 1013–14.

2. M. Bloch, 'Réflexions d'un historien sur les fausses nouvelles de la guerre', (1921) in *Melanges Historiques*, I, pp. 55–56, quoted in R. R. Davies, 'Marc Bloch', *History*, lii, 1967, p. 272.

3. C. Lévi-Strauss, *Structural Anthropology* (English translation, New York, 1963), pp. 167–85. I owe this reference to Dr. S. M. Lukes, of Balliol College, Oxford.

4. K. B. McFarlane, 'Bastard Feudalism', *Bulletin of the Institute of Historical Research*, xx, 1945, p. 178.

5. V. H. Galbraith, 'Good Kings and Bad Kings in English Medieval History', *History*, xxx, 1945, pp. 123–5.

6. For a discussion of this topic, see A. B. White, *Self-Government at the King's Command* (Minneapolis, 1933).

7. G. Barraclough, *The Medieval Empire: Idea and Reality* (Historical Association Pamphlet, 1950), especially pp. 20–4.

8. J. le Patourel, 'The Plantagenet Dominions', *History*, L, 1965, pp. 289–308.

9. T. F. Tout, *France and England, their relations in the middle ages and now* (Manchester, 1922), p. 162.

10. *Opere di Dante Alighieri* (ed. E. Moore and P. Toynbee, Oxford, 1894), pp. 383–4. There are various English translations of *De Vulgari Eloquentia:* the most accessible is the Temple Classics edition, 1904.

5

Early Modern History

Austin Woolrych

To the question 'why study history?' two sound answers
are commonly given. The first is that without it we cannot
fully comprehend the world we live in; the dimension of
time is essential to an understanding of the institutions,
the social structures, the unconsciously inherited habits of
thought which make up our human environment. Even if
we want to change them all, we need to know how they
came to be what they are. Professor Perkin has discussed
the values and limitations of this approach to history in
Chapter 1. An equally valid justification of the subject lies,
as Dr Tuck has rightly claimed in the last chapter, in the
value of studying periods that are profoundly different
from our own. If we raise our sights above our own particular predicament, if we seek a little wisdom about the human
condition in general, we can learn a great deal about the
astonishingly varied potential of man as a political and
social animal by absorbing ourselves in peoples and periods
whose ways of life and modes of thought are quite unlike
ours. By stretching our imagination upon the evidences they
have left behind, we free ourselves from a kind of parochialism, for there is a parochialism of time as well as place.

A study of the early modern period serves both these
valid purposes that history can claim. Compared with the
middle ages, its links with the present are more obvious and
it is more easily approachable. The geographical frontiers
are somewhat more recognizable, and more extensive; the
institutions of central and local government, at any rate

E

in England, look more like our own. The English landscape
is fast taking on its familiar pattern of hedged or walled
fields. As for buildings, splendid though the medieval heritage is in cathedrals, parish churches, abbeys and castles,
the sixteenth and seventeenth centuries have bequeathed a
vastly larger number of still inhabited houses—not only
the mansions of the nobility and squirearchy but countless
farms and small manor houses and town dwellings, the
sturdy products of the Great Rebuilding. Most of the literature of the age is open to us without a knowledge of Latin
or of early vernacular dialects, even though Latin was still
the language of More's *Utopia,* Camden's *Britannia,* Milton's larger prose works, and the seminal philosophical or
scientific treatises of Bacon, Spinoza and Newton. The music
of Dowland and Monteverdi and Purcell speaks to us far
more immediately than the angular sonorities of the high
middle ages—and what a close spiritual affinity links Britten
to Purcell, and Tippett to the Elizabethan madrigalists!

Yet in many respects the early modern period stands
closer to the medieval and further from our own than many
a university entrant who has 'done' Tudors or Stuarts at A-
level seems to realize. Some give themselves away by using
expressions like 'the masses', 'the man in the street', 'the
working classes', 'the rising middle class', and so on. The
language of class is largely meaningless when applied to
a society as small and scattered as that of pre-industrial
England, except so far as we can talk of a single governing
class composed of nobles, knights, esquires, and those leaders
of the more considerable urban communities who aspired
to the status of gentry. The essential unit, not only of society
but of production, was the family, and any solidarity a
man might feel with others of his own occupation or income-
group elsewhere generally mattered less immediately to him
than his relations with those just above and below him in
his local community. Population was still on a medieval
scale. That of England and Wales was somewhere around
three and a quarter million when Henry VIII died—less
than it had probably been at the end of the thirteenth
century. After another hundred years, at the time of the

Civil War, it may have increased by half, but it was still overwhelmingly rural and agrarian. London was by then the great exception, rising from perhaps a quarter to over half a million inhabitants in the course of the seventeenth century, by which time it was probably the biggest city in the world and nearly ten times larger than when Henry VII won the throne. But outside London only a tiny handful of towns reached the 10,000 mark in Tudor England, and probably only four (Bristol, Norwich, York and Southampton) exceeded 25,000 when Gregory King made his famous calculations of populations in 1688. The great majority of Englishmen lived in villages or still smaller settlements and drew their living, directly or indirectly, from the land. Perhaps six out of seven had their homes in communities of less than a thousand souls, and outside the small governing class the majority lived out their lives without ever seeing a town as we understand the term.

Not only in their numbers but in their typical occupations did the men of Tudor and Stuart England stand closer to their medieval forbears than to us. Villeinage was almost extinct, it is true; agrarian relationships, like the rural landscape, had changed far and were changing further, but in the laborious methods whereby hundreds of thousands of small husbandmen wrung a subsistence from the soil the changes were fewer. 'Manufacture' still normally meant the craftsman's shop and home. The roads too were mostly as bad as ever, and communications almost as slow as when Chaucer's pilgrims rode to Canterbury. Nor was the expectation of life much longer, for mortality, especially infant mortality, still ran high. There were of course no antiseptics and no anaesthetics, and the treatment prescribed by physicians, surgeons and apothecaries varied from the quaint to the terrifying. The plague was a visitation to be dreaded several times in an average lifetime, from the Black Death of 1348-9 right through to the Great Plague of 1665.

The most important political bond of medieval society was the feudal relationship between lord and vassal, with the king as the supreme feudal lord to whom all the rest owed allegiance. Feudalism had changed, in practice and in spirit. The tie between lord and man that had normally been based on the tenure of land gave way to the 'bastard feudalism' that rested only on a cash nexus or on a shifting calculation of mutual advantage. But between this stage, characteristic of the fifteenth century, and the relationship between client and patron that permeated early modern Europe, there was a strong line of continuity. The instinct that drove Elizabethan knights and squires to seek patronage of great nobles or courtiers or ministers of the crown, and impelled the latter to measure their standing by the strength of their 'clientage', was at bottom the same as had built up dangerous power groups round the leading magnates in the Wars of the Roses. Patronage as exercised by a Leicester, a Burghley or a Buckingham was very like bastard feudalism with the teeth drawn, in that it no longer de-manded service in arms, or a wholesale perversion of justice in the mutual interest of patron and client. But the teeth were not always drawn; Edward VI's reign in England saw a disquieting recrudescence of the overmighty subject, and the French Wars of Religion a far worse one. The vast *clientèles* that the houses of Guise and Montmorency and Bourbon gathered to themselves were not so different in essence from the magnate factions that had fought the Wars of the Roses in England. Loyalty was still intensely personal, and every prince in Europe had a struggle to make his subjects put their obedience to the state before their allegiance to their immediate lord or patron. Those who succeeded did so not by depersonalizing loyalty but by adequately embodying its object (the state) in their own persons; those who failed, like the sons of Catherine de Medici in France or the early Stuarts in England, were such as lacked the instinctive skills and temperament for this semi-mystical role. Even the English Civil War, which involved more obvious clashes of principle than most early modern conflicts, witnessed a fascinating series of gradations between traditional personal loyalties and devotion to a more abstract cause.

Dr Tuck has rightly stressed the intense self-conscious-ness and cohesion of local communities in the middle ages, but he would recognize how strongly they retained it in the early modern period. England was a more unified national state than most, but when a gentleman talked of his 'country', even in the seventeenth century, he more often than not meant Cornwall or Suffolk or whatever other shire formed the framework for his social life and his public service. 'In many respects,' writes Professor Everitt, 'the England of 1640 resembled a union of partly independent county-states or communities, each with its own distinct ethos and loyalty.'[1] Some of the most fruitful researches of recent years have concentrated on the gentry of a single county. These communities were less dominated than they had been by one or two great magnates with very large holdings of land; they were ruled now by a much broader range of landed families, holding commissions from the crown as justices of the peace, deputy lieutenants, sheriffs and so on, but regional loyalties and regional interests were as strong as ever. And if they remained so in England, how much more formidable they were in France, where the outlying provinces were only partially and precariously assimilated. The French Wars of Religion manifested such an explosive reaction of regional particularism that the kingdom was almost dismembered, and the Revolt of the Netherlands began in an effort not to launch a new nation-state but to save ancient provincial liberties.

I have stressed these continuities with the medieval past because it is from this background that we should approach the momentous developments of the early modern period, rather than from any narrow search for 'origins' of this or that phenomenon of our own time. To illustrate the point with one more example, anyone who has read E. M. W. Tillyard's *The Elizabethan World Picture* knows how much closer we get to Shakespeare's thought and images if we acquaint ourselves with the strange but coherent delineation of the universe that the Elizabethans inherited from the middle ages. Nor is this just a matter of literary appreciation, for the cosmology that depicted the heavenly bodies as held in concentric crystalline spheres in an ascending order of purity and incorruptibility, and ranged the various orders of angels in higher or lower degree, was often invoked to justify the social and political hierarchy on earth. The laws and customs that subordinated men to one another according to a strict scale of social status were part of the law of nature and the law of God, and it is only when we grasp what a commonplace this was that we can gauge how revolutionary were the egalitarian doctrines that the Levellers propagated in the 1640s.

History is bedevilled by the foolish antithesis between medieval and modern, suggesting as it does that the last thousand years or more can be carved into two contrasted eras, each more or less of a piece. Few discussions are less profitable than those we still meet with, about when the middle ages ended and the modern world began. We need at least a tripartite division of the time-span of western civilization since the dark ages, with the central period beginning earlier than the label 'early modern' usually implies, and standing forth more clearly in its own distinctive colours. Still, even if we give this intermediate age a shorter span than most of its historians would advocate—say from the mid-fifteenth century to the end of the seventeenth—what tremendous new departures and widenings of the horizon it exhibits, to set beside those continuities with the past that I have dwelt on so far! Here I can do little more than sketch a few of its great themes, some of which will be very familiar, some less familiar, to students who have worked on it at school. The difficulty is to know where to begin.

In the long term of history, it may be that nothing in this period affected the future of the world more crucially than the expansion of the western European nations into continents that had been unknown to the middle ages, or known only by the tales of rare travellers. The conquests that fastened an Iberian culture upon Central and South America were followed by settlements, tiny at first, that were to make the English language and English institutions of law and government the foundation-stone of a North American civilization which is now the greatest single power in world politics. At the same time the Dutch were staking

their claims in southern Africa, and the Portuguese defend-
ing more precarious footholds in Brazil, the coasts of Africa
and the Indian Ocean. Although Australia's and New Zea-
land's turns were still to come, the long dominance of a
basically European culture over most of the rest of the
known world was already assured.

Yet this European ascendancy could not have been won
and maintained without a steadily increasing superiority
in ship-building, navigation, weapons of war and techniques
of colonial exploitation. Very obviously, what most distinguishes our own culture from that of any previous civilization in world history is its technology. Less obviously,
the critical point of departure for our historically unique
power to control the world of nature lay in the scientific
revolution of the sixteenth and seventeenth centuries. That
picture of the universe which lent so many lovely images
to Elizabethan literature, with its heavenly spheres revolv-
ing around a stationary earth and its endowment of in-
animate matter with all kinds of instinctive attractions and
repulsions, was of course already under challenge in Shakespeare's time. But it took a lot of shaking, not only because
its explanations had proved satisfactory for so many centuries, but because the authority of the ancients on which it
rested—Aristotle, Ptolemy, Galen and the rest—was regarded
by conservatives as all but sacrosanct. The breakthrough
came only when bold men cleared their minds of the medieval cosmos and its world of spirits, and began to put new
questions to the material universe—questions whose answers
could be tested by experiment, measured in quantitative
terms, or extrapolated from the known data by the rapidly
developing art of mathematics. Without this forging of the
intellectual tools there could have been no technological revolution in the next age. There is a chapter later in this book on
the history of science, but one must mention it here because
nothing that happened in our period was more ultimately
important, and school and even university syllabuses are
apt to pass it by with a brief nod.

To many students, the early modern age is almost sum-
med up in those two vast phenomena, the Renaissance and

the Reformation, and they may be wondering why I have not referred to them earlier. Call it sheer funk if you like, but it really is difficult to say anything meaningful about them in a few paragraphs. One thing is certain: the undergraduate who studies them will have to clear his mind of many hoary generalizations which still pass for currency in the older textbooks, such as that the Renaissance ushered in the modern world, or that it derived its impetus from the fall of Constantinople in 1453. The Renaissance was a distinctive phase of civilization whose assumptions and values were very different from our own, and any adequate study of it must carry one considerably further back than the conventional boundaries between 'medieval' and 'early modern'. It is a subject that particularly calls for the interdisciplinary approach that some modern universities are developing so promisingly, for it demands the combined skills of historians of art, of philosophy, of politics and of political thought.

As for the Reformation, there is no need to emphasize the catastrophic effect of the huge breaches in the unity of christendom that were opened in the course of the sixteenth century. Again it is necessary to try to comprehend them through the minds of contemporaries, and that means learning something about the questions of faith and church government for which men fought and faced martyrdom. To study the Reformation in ignorance of these is almost like pursuing a course in the literature of a country whose language one cannot read. One does not have to be a believer to follow with absorption and even emotion the struggles of Lutherans and Calvinists, Anabaptists and Puritans, Catholic reformers and Jesuit missionaries, but one does have to grasp what they were contending about and how their actions followed upon their beliefs and premises. There are few more stultifying assumptions than that religious controversies were mere rationalizations of the interests of political power groups or economic classes. Fortunately, collections of contemporary texts, translated where necessary, are appearing in increasing numbers to make the student's task easier.

Less familiar than the Reformation, but scarcely less significant as a watershed in history, was the military revolution that took place roughly between 1560 and 1660.[2] It was only in this period that the tactical implications of field and siege artillery and of hand firearms were fully worked out. Once infantrymen were armed on any scale with muskets and cavalrymen with pistols or carbines, a much higher degree of training became necessary if these slow-loading, erratic weapons were to be used effectively on the battlefield. They demanded an increasingly elaborate drill, and the heavy investment in training-time and in weapons caused governments increasingly to keep their armies in being through the winter season and in time of peace. The days when untrained men could be impressed for a particular campaign and led by noblemen with only rudimentary military skills were rapidly passing. Armies not only became permanent but grew much larger, and demanded a growing machinery of state to arm, clothe, house, supply and generally administer them. England was the last major power to succumb to the need for a standing army and a large military establishment, but the wars of William III's and Anne's reigns finally forced her the way of her continental neighbours.

The professionalization of war and the growth of standing armies are intimately connected with another major phenomenon of early modern times: the growth in the power and organization of the state, and in particular the development of absolute monarchy. Standing armies were desperately expensive, and war provided the strongest motive for princes to override the consent of their parliaments or diets in raising revenue. Once established, military forces could too easily be used to cow any opposition to the levy of taxes, whether voted or not; the vicious circle is seen specially clearly in many parts of seventeenth-century Germany.

The fate of representative institutions is one of the most important themes of the whole period. In the fifteenth century, nearly every prince in Europe had to a greater or lesser extent to consult the estates of the realm, meaning normally a constitutional body representing the nobles, clergy and commons. In this there was a strong family likeness between most monarchies of the time, for this tempering of autocracy by the consent of the estates (parliament, diet, states-general, cortes, etc.) marks a long and important stage in the evolution of typical European government from medieval feudal kingship to the bureaucratized absolutisms of the eighteenth century. One of the absorbing questions is why representative institutions triumphed through many vicissitudes in Britain and the United Provinces, and survived in Aragon, Saxony, Württemberg, Poland and elsewhere, while in Castile, France, Bavaria, Brandenburg and Denmark, to take only a few examples, they succumbed to the new Leviathan. The answers vary in each particular state, but two factors keep recurring: the pressures of war, and the degree of subordination imposed by the social structure of the country in question. Whatever the causes and outcome, this constant conflict between constitutionalism and absolutism has left deep marks upon the political traditions of the nation-states of today. It is a most valuable object of study, and it calls for comparative treatment of a kind that is too often frustrated in sixth-form work by the strait jacket of the A-level syllabus.

I shall conclude by drawing back from the wide perspective of these last few pages and focusing again on English political history. I began by stressing its continuity with the medieval past; I end by indicating some ways in which it is different from medieval history, not just in content but in the way in which it can be written. I shall not discuss the vexed question whether Henry VIII's great minister Thomas Cromwell instituted a revolution in government; what is beyond doubt is that this reign, and particularly Cromwell's decade of power, witnessed something like a revolution in the records that the government kept of its activities. A quite dramatic enrichment of the source material makes the writing of political history possible on a fuller, more detailed scale than ever before—and one of the ways in which university work differs from school work lies in the interest that the undergraduate is expected

66

to take in at least some of the sources. In Thomas Cromwell's time, and indeed shortly before, the bald and stereo-
typed parchment records of the Chancery, the Privy Seal
Office, the Exchequer and other older departments of government recede in importance before a flood of paper of all
shapes and sizes. These 'state papers' are a new form of
public record. Mostly they emanate from the office of the
King's Principal Secretary, a post which Cromwell raised
to the highest political importance, and which would soon
change its name to Secretary of State. They include not
only all his correspondence and transactions on behalf of
the king (such as was safe to commit to paper, or to keep),
and not only the hundreds of letters and reports that he
received; they also reflect much of the activity of the Privy
Council. They give us a picture of a government more dynamic than ever before, extending the scope of its action,
pushing its tentacles ever deeper into the affairs of the
whole community of the realm, and dealing with a population that in its upper reaches was far more literate and
articulate than in the middle ages.

From 1540 the Acts of the Privy Council provide detailed
minutes of its daily proceedings, and seven years later the
Journals of the House of Commons begin. The Journals
are bare at first, but by Elizabeth's reign some M.P.s are
jotting notes of the debates on little pads on their knees—
enabling Sir John Neale to write the story of some of the
great conflicts in Elizabethan parliaments almost as though
he had a shelf of Hansard before him and had dined with a
leading member or two in his club.[3]

And here is another great difference that enters our history
roughly with the Tudor period : the far greater vividness
with which its prominent personalities come through. As
Dr Tuck has remarked, medieval chroniclers knew only a
limited range of personalities; a few trite judgments, a few
conventional virtues or villainies, are all that they commonly give us. But Tudor writers, and still more those of
the seventeenth century, were tremendously interested in
personality. It was thanks partly to the Renaissance cult of
the classical historians, with their absorption in the conflict

between great characters and the brute circumstances that they wrestled with. Sir Thomas More, for example, stands before us revealed in a humanity and a complexity of character unprecedented. For this we have chiefly to thank his son-in-law William Roper for writing an intimate biography of him, but we owe something too to Erasmus, who described More's home life in a famous epistle to Ulrich von Hutten, and not a little to the brush and crayon of Holbein. Contemporary biographies multiply as the sixteenth century advances, and by the early seventeenth the 'character', a short piece not unlike the 'profiles' in our Sunday papers, has become a recognized literary *genre*. Two of the most enjoyable collections are Aubrey's *Brief Lives*[4] and Thomas Fuller's *Worthies of England,* both delightfully alert to human idiosyncracies and curious about the mainsprings of human action.

By the time of Aubrey and Fuller we can often get a unified view of political events through the memoirs of men who were intimately engaged in them, such as Edmund Ludlow, Bulstrode Whitelocke and Richard Baxter in the time of the Great Rebellion. Occasionally a great actor on the political stage attempted a sustained interpretation in a work of full-scale contemporary history. Clarendon's *History of the Rebellion*[5] is the greatest example, with its superb gallery of pen-portraits, but for sheer unbuttoned readability we must save a mention for Bishop Gilbert Burnet's *History of His Own Time.* The age is also rich in that still more intimate form of record, the diary; Archbishop Laud's is only one example of outstanding historical value. As for personal letters, the riches grow with each decade. In the last hundred years the Royal Commission for Historical Manuscripts has published over two hundred volumes containing selections from over four hundred private collections —and there are many more waiting to be tapped in the County Records Offices and the archives of noble mansions.

Finally (though this selection is all too arbitrary), there are those often illicit offspring of the new printing presses, the pamphlets. From the first Reformation tracts through the barbed satires of Martin Marprelate's assaults on the bishops to the great controversies of the Civil War and the Commonwealth, pamphlets take us into the heart of the ideological clashes of the age by preserving the words of men who were prepared to risk imprisonment and worse in an effort to persuade an unknown public through the printed word. One great collection must suffice as an example. A London bookseller named George Thomason, the friend of Milton and Prynne among others, resolved when the Long Parliament met to collect every tract that he could buy on the bookstalls. He continued until the coronation of Charles II twenty years later, and the British Museum still holds over 22,000 items that he amassed. His collection is an inestimable treasury for all who seek to recover the ideas and ideals for which men strove in England's one major political revolution. No wonder that American as well as British scholars descend on it in swarms when the universities' vacations give them a chance to pursue their researches.

The early modern period has undergone more reappraisals in the last generation than this brief essay could possibly convey. It still bristles with unsolved problems; it remains as rich in its intellectual challenges as in the enormously varied sources from which the answers wait to be worked out.

SUGGESTED READING

ELTON, G. R. (ed.), *Renaissance and Reformation, 1300–1648*, (Collier-Macmillan paperback, 2nd ed., 1968).

LASLETT, PETER, *The World We Have Lost* (Methuen University Paperbacks, 1965).

PARRY, J. H., *The Age of Reconnaissance* (Mentor Books, paperback, 1964).

DICKENS, A. G., *Reformation and Society in Sixteenth-Century Europe* (Thames & Hudson paperback, 1966).

TILLYARD, E. M. W., *The Elizabethan World Picture* (Chatto & Windus, 1943; Peregrine paperback, 1963).

NEALE, J. E., *The Elizabethan House of Commons* (1949; Peregrine paperback, 1963).

HEXTER, J. H., *Reappraisals in History* (Longmans, 1961).

STONE, LAWRENCE, *Social Change and Revolution in England, 1540–1640* (Longmans paperback, 1965).

IVES, E. W. (ed.), *The English Revolution, 1600–1660* (Arnold paperback, 1968).

CHAPTER NOTES

1. Alan Everitt, *The Community of Kent and the Great Rebellion, 1640–1660* (Leicester U.P., 1966), p. 13. See also Everitt's excellent pamphlet, *The Local Community and the Great Rebellion* (Historical Association, 1969), which surveys the whole subject and lists the best of the recent work on it.

2. See Michael Roberts' brilliant paper on 'The Military Revolution, 1560–1660', reprinted in his *Essays in Swedish History* (Weidenfeld and Nicolson, 1967).

3. J. E. Neale, *Elizabeth I and Her Parliaments* (2 vols., Cape, 1953–1957).

4. More fun to read in the unexpurgated edition by O. Lawson Dick (Secker & Warburg, 1949). For a good anthology, see *Characters of the Seventeenth Century*, ed. David Nichol Smith (Clarendon Press, 1918).

5. An excellent selection by Gertrude Huehns from this very large work is published by the Oxford University Press in the World's Classics edition.

6

Modern British
Political History

David Hamer

A question that is often asked by University students of
History is why there is so much emphasis on one particular
area of historical study—the history of their own country.
The most obvious answer is, of course, that it is in this
area of study that we come closest to gaining an understanding of ourselves, of the social and cultural conditions
which have helped to create the fabric of our own everyday
lives. The need to understand, so as to be able to control,
live with, and change, our environment is of vital importance for all of us. No such understanding is possible unless
we have investigated the processes by which that environment has been formed. The organic reality of the phenomena
and attitudes of the present is the product of the past.
The present is merely a transitory instant of time that is
constantly becoming the past; the future we do not and
cannot know about. The past *is* the reality of human existence, and it is the task of the historian to investigate and
analyse it and tell us not only what men were and did but
what *we are* and how our social actions are circumscribed
and affected by a multitude of decisions and failures to make
decisions, of movements and tendencies.

There is also the fact that we are simply able to know
and understand more about the history of our own country.
The material is much more accessible, and the language
is our own, so that we do not have to rely on second-hand

acquaintance with the primary sources through the medium of translation or our own acquired knowledge of a foreign language. Furthermore, in our own country the scholars are most numerous in this area of historical investigation. Thus the student who enters it finds himself particularly close to the making of history.

The second feature of the history which is the subject of this chapter is that it is political; and in this respect too the historian can find himself on the defensive, troubled perhaps by a guilty feeling that he is writing and thinking only about a very small proportion of the population—the politicians and leading opinion-formers—while neglecting 'real' history, economic and social, that is concerned with the lives of the mass of people. Certainly, 'history' and political history very often have appeared to be synonymous for historians and organizers of university courses. This emphasis on the political aspects of man's past is easily explained. This is the kind of history which has been always most copiously and officially recorded and preserved. It is in this area more than any other that there is concern for the keeping of records and the preserving of documents.

What one has to be aware of above all, however, is the artificiality of all divisions of historical study. It is almost impossible to write 'pure' political history. Even the study of political intrigue is incomplete unless the social situations of the participants are taken into account. The political historian can make little sense of the political events which he describes and analyses unless he is aware of the wider context of these events, intellectual, social, and economic. He needs to consider the basic assumptions and the general climate of opinion in the period about which he is writing so that he can appreciate more accurately why politicians behaved in certain ways, i.e. what instincts or deep-rooted assumptions shared by them with their contemporaries shaped their response to particular political crises. He needs to consider the section of society from which a politician comes and how he came from it, whether by patronage or via party organization, for example. He needs to take account of all the social influences surrounding a politician and affecting his conduct, influences many of which the politician himself will have been barely, if at all, conscious of. Politicians are confronted with concrete social problems. We have to find out as much as possible about these ourselves so that we can assess to what extent a particular politician knew or understood what was going on.

Historians find that, whatever area or type of history they have a special interest in, it impinges substantially on the subject-matter of at least one non-historical field of study. Thus those of us who work in modern British political history find that it is difficult—and of course often undesirable—to establish clear lines of distinction between our work and that of our colleagues whose subject is politics. The line of academic demarcation which seems most commonly to be assumed is that politics is about 'the present' whereas we historians ought to confine our investigations to 'the past'. All such divisions are artificial, and in particular, as I suggested above, the term, 'the present', has little meaning. The student of politics cannot help but 'go back' even five or ten years if he is investigating some present-day political institution. The student of recent history, on the other hand, often wonders what criteria determine when 'history' ought to stop. This is a particular problem with modern British history. Should courses go down 'to the present day' or stop in 1951 or 1964? Is it the availability of certain kinds of source material, e.g. private papers, which determines whether or not a certain topic can be treated 'historically'?

It might be argued that the student of politics is not so interested in dead ends. Those features of the politics of the past which somehow failed to survive to the present day in recognizable form are left to the historian. An example is Robert McKenzie's *British Political Parties* where the organizational history of the Liberal party in the nineteenth century is given less attention than an historian of the party system might feel is warranted.

The political historian, if he is wise, ignores all such academic distinctions. Writers on politics such as J. P. Mack-

73

intosh (*The British Cabinet*) and S. H. Beer (*Modern British Politics*) provide new insights into British political history because they approach it from a different standpoint. What the historian normally has to offer is a much closer, more detailed acquaintance with the source material of political history. Books on politics sometimes seem historically superficial and inadequate because they rely so much for their 'historical' material on the generalizations to be found in basic text-books.

There are various problems associated with the study of the recent political history of one's own country. It is perhaps the area of historical study from which one is and can be least detached emotionally and in regard to the circumstances of one's own life, the area in which personal prejudices and attitudes are bound to be most strongly involved. The mind which a student brings to it is no *tabula rasa* but is already filled with a mass of notions, mostly best described as folklore or myths, about the history of the community in which he lives. We naturally feel that we know and understand a great deal already simply by virtue of being members of that society; much of our academic work in history may turn out to be destructive, therefore, in the sense of undermining certainties and sowing numerous seeds of doubt. With the history of some other country, say China, by contrast, a student starts not only in a state of total ignorance but *knowing* that he is in such a state.

Another complicating factor about the study of the history of one's own country is that there are so many lines extending from it into 'the present'—so much business that is still unfinished, so many problems that are still awaiting solutions and issues that remain alive and subjects of current controversy. The political parties between which we have to choose and concerning the policies of which we are likely to have strong views have been in existence for a considerable time, and it is not easy to switch from a committed, contemporary viewpoint to one that is more analytical and 'objective'. Furthermore, in the very act of analysing these issues and problems and political phenomena we are helping to influence contemporary debate by placing them

74

in a different perspective. The great danger here, of course, is that we will concentrate on and think important and 'relevant' only those questions which are still with us. We will select only those topics which remind us of issues which are alive in our own time and will thus distort the record of the past to reflect the current state of opinion. This is a danger in all areas of historical study, even those very distant from our own time: we tend naturally to look for and concentrate on themes that seem to be related to issues in which we are interested in the contemporary world. But with 'recent history' it is obviously a particularly difficult problem to come to grips with. How hard it is, for instance, for us to place in historical perspective or to judge solely in terms of the period the 'appeasement' policies of the British government in the 1930s! Again and again since 1945 politicians have referred to the alleged wrongness of these policies as justification for a particular course of policy which they themselves have wished to follow—whether preparation for armed resistance to the 'advance of Russian Communism' in Europe, or Eden's Suez policy in 1956, or the involvement of the United States in the war in Vietnam. Another example would be the Ulster issue on which we, as contemporary citizens of the United Kingdom, may have strong views which could affect our assessment of the situation, say, in 1886 or 1914.

Interpretations of recent British political history undoubtedly form a very important part of the climate of opinion in our society. Politicians are constantly offering us as explanation of what they are doing or proposing to do their version of what happened in the past. The ideas which they put forward are very rarely accurate or objective assessments—and, of course, are not intended to be. They represent what the politicians *want us* to think about the past, and they are advanced, not as a contribution to historical understanding—for to offer such contributions is not the job of the politican—but in order to influence our reaction to what the politicians are doing at the present time. There are many ideas about British history which comprise what could be called the folklore of our society, myths

75

that survive and are generalized as the lowest common denominators out of the infinitely complex process of reaction and judgement produced by any major historical event. These myths often conflict: for instance, Conservative and Labour party members have sharply contrasting ideas about the nature of each party. The politician himself, in telling his audiences what 'happened' in the past, will in part instinctively draw on this heritage and in part consciously select those aspects of it which seem most likely to serve his current purpose. But in his turn, because of the great amount of attention which is paid to what he says, he will do much to create or to harden popular misconceptions and myths. Nor is it only the politician who thus influences society's view of what happened in its past. Political commentators in the newspapers or on television, striving to simplify for mass audiences or connect with their prejudices and instincts, and in any case usually needing to produce assessments very quickly, also rely on, and do much to give renewed and widened currency to, these myths.

We therefore find that as students of modern British political history, with no axe to grind, no ulterior political motive to promote, we are, in spite of, and also to a large extent because of, our detachment from contemporary passions and preoccupations, making a significant contribution to contemporary debate. We are not producing the complete 'truth', the definitive interpretation, of any aspect of the past, for no historian can ever do that, given the fragmentary nature of the evidence which has survived for us from the past. But we are trying to assess the past in a different way and in its own terms, not the terms dictated by present-day political exigencies or obsessions. What we find and say may never reach the general public, or may do so only in the highly simplified form of the text-book or the work of popularization, to help in the creation of new myths or modifications of old ones. But the student of history himself becomes a countervailing influence in the formation of opinion in our society—of opinion not about a past that is dead and forgotten but of a past which extends into and is constantly absorbing 'the present'.

As I observed above, one sometimes hears the argument that political history is less 'real', less 'important' than, say, social or economic history because its concern is only with politicians, a very small proportion of the population. It may be that at one time this argument, and the distinction implied in it between incompatible categories of history, had some validity. But the British social historian no longer attempts, as did G. M. Trevelyan, to write social history as history with the politics left out: he takes very full account of politics, as does Professor Perkin in his *Origins of Modern English Society* for instance, as, *inter alia,* a form of social behaviour, a reflection of and vehicle for social attitudes and wants, and a response to social pressures and social change. And anyone who is familiar with recent work in modern British political history would recognize as a travesty of the real situation the claim that political historians now concern themselves only with professional politicians. Much history now concerns the attitudes and political behaviour of the mass of people, of those who do not govern but are the concern of those who do. It is now recognized that political and social history cannot satisfactorily be studied in separate compartments, that the behaviour even of the professional politicians is rooted in, and cannot be understood without reference to, a particular social structure, and that 'politics' *can* be a study which involves analysis of the attitudes and conduct of masses of people.

Of course, evidence on which to base this kind of investigation into political history is much harder to come by, much less carefully preserved, and much less readily intelligible. This is no doubt why in the past so little has been done on it. One notes now, for instance, the material used by E. P. Thompson in his *Making of the English Working Class* or G. Rudé in *Wilkes and Liberty*—court records and reports of police spies, popular literature, broadsheets, etc.

'The people' come formally into the political process when a general election is held, and the study of elections is naturally an important part of the study of modern political

77

history. The material available for it varies considerably from period to period. In the unreformed parliamentary system, and indeed in most constituencies down to 1867, electorates were very small, and there were individuals with the means, whether it was wealth or social influence, of controlling voting, which was 'open' until 1872. It is quite easy therefore to reconstruct in detail the process whereby a pre-1867 Parliament was formed. Furthermore, pollbooks for many constituencies still survive from the pre-1872 era (see John Vincent, *Pollbooks: How Victorians Voted,* Cambridge, 1967). These show how registered voters cast their votes and provide us with useful, if complex, evidence as to, for instance, the relationship between occupation and support for particular parties. But with the advent of the secret ballot in 1872 the veil descends. The period 1872-1945 is the most mysterious in British electoral history. The basic unit is the constituency, the population of which, except in a few areas such as mining districts, is usually heterogeneous. Within each constituency the spread of votes as between one social class and another or among different occupations can only be guessed at: all votes are collected together and counted in one place. Since 1945, however, some of the mystery that surrounds the whole question of electoral behaviour has been lifting, mainly on account of opinion polls and the development of more or less sophisticated techniques of sociological inquiry and analysis. (For examples, see R. McKenzie and A. Silver, *Angels in Marble: Working Class Conservatives in Urban England* (1968), and E. A. Nordlinger, *The Working-Class Tories* (1967). One result of this analysis has been to highlight the question of the effect and importance of election campaigns themselves—and to make us look more at long-term trends and the role of permanent interests than at dramatic short-term changes of fortune.

A great deal of political history is concerned with ideas and 'opinion'. In trying to reconstruct what happened in the past, we have to keep in mind that much of our evidence has to be classified as opinion rather than fact. We often construct political narrative from speeches and letters giving

men's views on what they think ought to be done or justifications of what has been done. In historical study opinions
are facts, the raw material of political life out of which
come decisions and actions. There are several levels at
which the political historian discovers and analyses 'thought'
and 'opinion' in the broader sense, that is underlying attitudes and assumptions which shape responses to political
situations:

(i)   the writings of great political philosphers or analysts,
      e.g. Carlyle, the Mills, T. H. Green, Walter Bagehot.
      The political historian will be particularly interested
      in the reasons for the popularity of the writings of
      these men and will examine the ways in which they
      represented and also helped to form the main currents
      of thought of their time;

(ii) 'opinion'—the product of the incessant, day-by-day
      interchange of ideas in the press and on the platform
      (and in our own times on radio and television too);

(iii) what might be called assumptions or prejudices or
      instincts, which are seldom made articulate but which
      in fact guide political practice to a very considerable
      extent. We are interested, for example, in what are,
      and what has formed, the instincts by which a polit-
      ician, immersed in the flow of events and under con-
      stant pressure, has to allow himself to be guided.
      One has to look, for instance, at the characteristics of
      a man's social and regional situation in early life—
      Lloyd George and Wales, or Joseph Chamberlain and
      Birmingham, for example—and at the ideas current
      in his formative years more perhaps than those current
      in his years as an active politician, for his involvement
      in practical affairs may make him immune to the in-
      fluence of the latter. How a politician sees a political
      situation, indeed his most basic assumptions, can often
      be gauged by the kind of imagery which he uses in
      his speeches and writings;

(iv) popular attitudes: problems connected with discover-
      ing these are discussed above.

There are different ways in which political history can be written. One way is to try to present the flow of events as it appeared at the time to the participants. This is extremely difficult and can never be done in any more than a very fragmentary form because of the paucity of evidence available. The historian always needs to make a distinction between what was happening and what the participants thought was going on and to reconcile also the very different impressions of the same event which different participants can have. The political historian will try to become immersed in the flow of events so as to give himself some idea of what it was like to be Mr X or Lord Y faced with the necessity of making a certain decision in a certain set of circumstances and subject to certain pressures. The great problem for the historian is to remember that there was only so much that Mr X or Lord Y knew about what was going on, that what he thought he knew might have been distorted or inaccurate for a variety of reasons, and, above all, that he did not know what was going to happen subsequently. The historian knows both much more and much less than the men about whom he is writing. He must be careful in particular not to let his knowledge of the future get in the way of understanding the political conduct of individuals. Writing history so as to give the impression of politicians having to confront 'one damned thing after another', being involved in perpetual muddle and uncertainty, and having constantly to improvise and to discard 'best laid plans', can yield very fruitful results. Examples of recently published books that are written in this style are A. J. P. Taylor's volume in the Oxford History of England—a striking contrast with its formally structured and compartmented predecessors in that series—and Maurice Cowling's *1867: Disraeli, Gladstone and Revolution* (Cambridge, 1967).

Usually, however, the historian must also select and highlight, construct patterns and interpretations, and suggest what he believes was 'really' going on. He will show, for example, how a certain result—which *he* knows about—

was working itself out unknown to the persons who can now be seen as having helped to produce it.

The historian who wishes to reconstruct British politics of the recent past, to find out what went on behind the scenes, how decisions were arrived at or evaded, and what influences —unknown to the public at the time—caused politicians to behave in certain ways is very dependent on manuscript collections, the papers of leading politicians. Of those collections which have survived and which relate to careers before 1914 most are now in libraries and other institutions. Thus the British Museum now has the papers of, among many others, Gladstone, Peel, Aberdeen, Campbell-Bannerman, and Balfour. It is for more recent history that manuscript sources are hard to come by: families are often reluctant to open up to the public papers which may refer to people still living, and in any case papers need much careful sifting and ordering before they can be made available for general scholarly use.

That a collection of his papers exists is itself no guarantee that a great deal can as a result be known about a politician. The evidence which it provides can very often be only indirect: many collections consist mainly of letters *to* the men whose papers they are. Not often do politicians keep copies of their own letters. Consequently, one collection on its own is usually not enough to form the basis of a study of a man's career and opinions. However, papers *are* a nucleus, and their existence can be an incentive to an historian to work on the man concerned. There is a certain mystique about manuscript collections. They are widely regarded as the highest form of evidence, and research scholars tend to keep away from men whose papers do not happen to have survived, even though diligent search through the collections of many other politicians may often turn up a large amount of the correspondence of such men. Whenever we read an analysis or interpretation which a political historian has arrived at after consulting manuscript collections, we must remember how fragmentary is and must be the impression which he gives us of the past. He has to use what has chanced to survive—a mere fragment of all that was written among the politicians with whom he is concerned. Papers have often been destroyed, by the politician himself perhaps, or by his heirs through ignorance of their historical significance or fear of possible embarrassment, or just by accidents, fire or bombing raids, for example. Except for those such as the great Whig aristocrats—e.g. the Spencers of Althorp, with whom the keeping of family archives in the 'muniments room' is a centuries-old tradition reflecting the family's hereditary political role—with politicians there has to be a positive will to see that papers are kept. Perhaps there has to be also a certain conceit, a feeling that posterity will, or ought to be, interested in what one has done. For otherwise papers can be quickly scattered and lost. How many of us keep all our letters anyway? It is common practice for people to throw letters away after reading them. How often, on the other hand, does the political historian bless the ignoring or overlooking by a recipient of a note such as this on a letter: 'Please burn when read'!

In spite of problems connected with getting access to departmental and Cabinet papers and private manuscript collections for the study of twentieth-century British political history, the researcher soon finds that a major problem is the sheer abundance of material available. This reflects two modern phenomena in particular: (i) the growth of literacy and the spread of education at all social levels, which has led to a vast proliferation of printed sources—newspapers, journals, pamphlets, and so on; and (ii) the growth of bureaucracy and of the power and interference of the State. Acts of Parliament and the incessant creation of new areas of activity for the State have generated vast masses of official records. Furthermore, since the early Victorian era governments have found it increasingly necessary to investigate social and economic conditions and accumulate information in order to have a reliable basis on which to take legislative and administrative action. Mistakes can be disastrous, to the state of society and of the economy as well as to the reputations of politicians and the tenure of office by political parties.

But in one area there has been a significant decline in

the amount of evidence available for the writing of political history. The introduction of the telephone has meant that politicians in the twentieth century communicate with one another to a very considerable extent in a form which leaves no trace behind it. The archives of pre-1914 politicians abound in messages—arranging meetings, planning strategy, inviting to dinner—of the kind which would now customarily be transmitted by telephone. As a result, it becomes much less easy, for example, to reconstruct a politician's movements and to find out with whom he was in contact at times of political crisis.

Another type of primary material which political historians use is politicians' memoirs. These are frequently unreliable. They are usually apologia written to justify what the author did and to put the various aspects and episodes of his career in the best possible light. He will select material with this end in mind. Furthermore, memoirs are usually written by old men after their public lives have ended, and 'old men forget'. Most memoirs are merely anecdotal, and except where letters and diaries are quoted—and these, of course, can be 'doctored' for publication—are of little value to the historian who is trying to reconstruct what happened *at the time*. There are also the official biographies, undertaken very often on commission from the family. These must be used with care. If written soon after a man's death, they tend to lack that historical perspective and all-round understanding such as can only come after much research into the situations in which he was involved has been undertaken. Particularly valuable are diaries. Very few politicians keep these; the outstanding example of one who did is Gladstone, whose diaries are now in the process of being published. Politicians lack time and usually also a certain fascination at being in the company of men 'greater' than oneself that is so often an ingredient in the mental state of a diarist. The most useful and interesting diaries tend to be those written by secondary figures—journalists, private secretaries, family friends—or by 'go-betweens', men who find their greatest pleasure in carrying messages and arbitrating between the great. For example, the historian of late nineteenth-century Liberalism is constantly quarrying the diaries of two men who acted at various times as Gladstone's private secretaries, Sir Algernon West and Sir Edward Hamilton. The latter's diaries have not been published, and over forty black-bound volumes in the British Museum furnish most valuable accounts of innumerable conversations with such men as Gladstone, Rosebery, Harcourt, and Lord Randolph Churchill.

The undergraduate studying history at the university soon finds that as an academic subject it is the creation of historians. Of necessity, because of his dependence on printed and secondary sources, the topics which he studies have to be those to which historians have happened to direct their attention. The study of history is the study of controversy, of the constant debate among historians as to what 'really' occurred in history and why. The student soon finds that certain issues are 'alive' because historians are researching into and provoking discussion and debate about them, while others lie dormant and neglected. Thus in modern British political history there is at the moment and has been for some time great interest in the origins and early years of the Labour party but much less in the history of the Liberal and Conservative parties in the late nineteenth century. Among other topics which have been the subject of much investigation, debate, and re-interpretation recently have been the extent to which the conservatism that developed in the 1790s was reactionary, the influence of fears or threats of revolution over the passing of the first and second Reform bills, the political influence of the Fabian Socialists, the causes of the decline of the Liberal party, and the political crisis of 1931. But these are only a few out of many. New evidence, new insights and viewpoints, new interpretations of old material, mean that there is a constantly changing landscape in the study of modern British political history. History in the sense of the deeds and thoughts of the past may be 'dead'; but in history as an academic subject these are converted into the substance of live controversy and inquiry.

SUGGESTED READING

BROOKE, J., *The Prime Ministers' Papers, 1801–1902* (Her Majesty's Stationery Office, 1968).

BUTTERFIELD, H., *George III and the Historians* (Collins, 1957).

KITSON CLARK, G., *The Making of Victorian England* (Methuen, 1962), Chapter I: 'The Task of Revision'.

COWLING, M., *1867: Disraeli, Gladstone and Revolution* (Cambridge University Press, 1967), Epilogue: 'The limitations of historical knowledge'.

PELLING, H., *Popular Politics and Society in late Victorian Britain* (Macmillan, 1968)—good examples of an historian's deflation of historical myths.

WATT, D. C. (ed.), *Contemporary History in Europe* (Allen and Unwin, 1969), Essays on Britain by R. Rhodes James and J. Barnes.

7

Social and Economic History

Harold Perkin

History, we saw in Chapter 1, is about the whole life of man in past society. Historians, even those concerned primarily with politics and war, have always had to take into account other factors, above all the industrial production and economic wealth of their chosen societies, which determined their capacity for war and politics, and their social structure and *mores,* which determined what they did with their economic resources and political power, their ideals of what life was for, who led and who followed, and often the issues of political and military conflict, not to say the unity and morale with which it was pursued. Thucydides in *The Peloponnesian War* had to describe the comparative social systems of Athens and Sparta in order to explain what the war was about. Julius Caesar felt it necessary to depict the manners and customs, the dress and religion of the wild and barbarous Britons that he came and saw and temporarily conquered. Tacitus was as much concerned with the agriculture and social organization of the German tribes as with their military threat to the Roman Empire, the Venerable Bede with the conversion of the English as with their conquests, Shakespeare (if we may admit a dramatic historian) with the moral state of Yorkist and Lancastrian England as with the civil wars which caused it to deteriorate. Coming nearer to our own day, Macaulay's famous third chapter is a social and economic account of England on the eve of the Glorious Revolution, Carlyle's *French Revolution* a passionate account of moral and spiritual conflict and corruption, A. V. Dicey's *Law and Opinion* a legal historian's view of the impact of ideas on social and economic legislation. In this century the dominant technique in political history has been the 'mass biography' of Sir Lewis Namier and Sir John Neale, which can best be described as the study of the social origins of politicians and the social roots of politics.

The political historian, however, with his preoccupation with political conflict and the constitutional framework within which it takes place, rarely has time for the systematic study of the economy and society, and so there has grown up a new species of specialists in economic and social history. In a sense their approach is as old as the modern study of political history, for it dates back to the eighteenth-century 'Scottish historical school of philosophy' which began the historical study of the social sciences, and culminated in Adam Smith's *Wealth of Nations* (1776), in effect the economic history of the 'mercantile system', and in his pupil John Millar's *Origin of the Distinction of Ranks* (1771), the first (if speculative) history of social structure. Their successors, the classical economists, however, turned away from historical explanation towards Ricardian abstraction, and it was not until the later Victorians, Thorold Rogers' *History of Agriculture and Prices* (1866-87) and the elder Arnold Toynbee's lectures on *The Industrial Revolution* (1884), that economic history revived. After that came, partly under the influence of the Victorian and Edwardian land reform movement, a flood of writing on agrarian history—Seebohm, Vinogradoff, Curtler, Slater, Johnson, Gray, the Hammonds and Tawney—and a smaller but still substantial stream on industry and trade—Archdeacon Cunningham, Sir William Ashley, Chapman, Unwin and the Webbs. Between the Wars economic history established itself in most British universities, though mostly in economics departments, and names like Unwin, Tawney, the Hammonds, the Coles, Eileen Power, Sir John Clapham, T. S. Ashton and Arthur Redford became as familiar to history students as those of Tout, Tait, Trevelyan, Neale and Namier.

Today economic history is an accepted part of practically

all social science degrees and of most history courses, whether it is taught as in most cases by the economics department, as in a minority by the history department, or as in a few by a department separate from both. Social history, where it is mentioned at all, is normally bracketed with economic. Only at Lancaster is there a separate established chair of social history (though there is a personal chair at Edinburgh and a chair of medieval social history at Birmingham), though not a separate department. This is not because it is not taught elsewhere. It is almost impossible to teach economic history without some social content. If economic history deals with the way men in the past earned their living and distributed and exchanged their products, these can hardly be dealt with adequately without some reference to the things they lived for and spent their livings on—family life, religion, education, fashion, art, pleasures and pastimes, and so on; to the quality as well as the quantity of that living, and the conditions in which they earned and spent it; and to the wider system of relationships of which those between landlord and tenant, employer and worker, buyer and seller, and so on, were merely part. The great pioneers of the subject were as much social as economic historians. Marx's economic interpretation is strictly a sociological one, since the class struggle depends as much on class consciousness as on economic interest. George Unwin's *Industrial Organization in the Sixteenth and Seventeenth Centuries* (Oxford, 1904) is a study of the revolution in the social structure of the craft gilds and industrial towns with the rise of the domestic outwork system, R. H. Tawney's *The Agrarian Problem of the Sixteenth Century* (1912) of the related revolution in rural society with the rise of modern commercial agriculture. Thus there are good precedents and good reasons for teaching economic and social history together.

There are also good reasons for teaching them separately. In social studies faculties no-one today would assume that a course in economics adequately covered sociology, or *vice versa*. Although they overlap and support each other, the economist would not consider that the sociologist

dealt with the economy systematically enough, the sociologist that the economist sufficiently dealt with the social
structure. In the same way the economic and the social
historian have different foci of interest, the one on the historical development of the economy, the other on that of the
social structure, and there is some danger that the major
interest may distract from or distort the minor. This has
happened in some very economic courses of economic history,
where the factors of production and the gross national
product almost exclude the study of the men and classes
which embody and produce them.

There is less danger of this happening the other way
round: since social history is the widest kind of history,
and must consider everything which affects the social structure, it cannot afford to neglect so vital an aspect as the
way in which each section of society earned its living, the
relative size of that living, and the special category of relationships (tenure, employment, usury, etc.) generated by
economic activities. The neglect, if any, is that of the landscape artist, who must bring in everything, including topo-
graphy, buildings and people, though some may be too
lightly sketched, over against that of the architectural
painter, who concentrates on the buildings and brings in
the landscape and the people only incidentally. The economic
like the political historian is a specialist who abstracts from
the total scene, the social historian a generalist whose
function is to depict the whole, but with a special interest
in composition and perspective. This comes out in their
writings, where the political or economic historian's approach
to general history is to add on a chapter on 'social life',
whereas the social historian brings in politics and economics, like religion, education or any other aspect, as and when
they are required, that is, when they affect his central theme,
the development of the social structure. For social history,
like sociology to the social sciences, provides the trunk on
which the other branches hang.

In practice, however, time in a three-year degree is too
short for mutually independent courses of social and economic history. The two are normally taught together, and

89

which one is the major focus of interest depends on the bias of the particular university teacher. Some see themselves as historical economists, using historical evidence to illustrate economic theories; others (though they are rarer in universities than in schools and book publishing) as historians of social life, concerned only with eating and drinking, fashions in dress and furniture, morals and manners, and the like; but the bulk of them see their task as that of describing and analysing both the way in which men in the past earned their living and how they lived at different levels of society in co-operation and/or conflict with each other. Both approaches imply some systematic study of the economic framework and the social structure; not primarily as social scientists searching out evidence to support abstract theory, but as historians concerned with the unique phenomena of particular past societies, which indeed are more valuable to the social scientist when studied as integral, working wholes to set alongside and compare with modern societies than when treated as quarries of illustrative facts torn out of their historical context.

Working together, they can be enormously illuminating, to the political or general historian as to the economist or sociologist. Medieval English history can scarcely be understood without some knowledge of the utter dependence of the bulk of the population on agriculture, and on agricultural techniques which, though poor by modern standards, were so immeasurably superior to those of the ancient Britons that they enabled the Anglo-Saxons to colonize the virgin forest and heavy clay soils and so to support a larger and militarily more powerful population. The major regional differences in agriculture, between the open-field area of the central lowlands running from Northumberland to the south coast and the enclosed lands to the south-east and to the north and west, had profound effects on the pattern of settlement—large, nucleated villages in the central belt, hamlets and scattered farms on either side—which are visible to the present day. But these differences in turn cannot be understood in terms of agricultural technique, geography and climate alone. They had some relation to differences in social custom and structure, and above all to their different customs of inheritance, the Anglo-Saxons in the centre practising primogeniture, inheritance by the eldest male heir, which kept the holdings together; the Britons of the north and west and the Jutes and Frisians of the South-east, partible inheritance, which tended to split up consolidated holdings into hamlets of descendants of a common ancestor.[1] The difference in social custom affected the very landscape, and not only in the form of open field versus 'old enclosure'. In the Lincolnshire fenland partible inheritance gave a small amount of the 'high land' and appurtenant rights in the fen to every son of a sokeman, which motivated the peasants to drain hundreds of square miles of saltmarsh and peat fen, and down to this day villages which had large numbers of sokemen have denser populations than their nextdoor neighbours.[2]

On Tudor and Stuart England economic and social history come together in the pioneering work of Unwin and Tawney, already mentioned. The rise of capitalist industry in the domestic outwork system and the rise of capitalist agriculture with large tenant farmers and landless labourers were connected, since the one supplied the other with labour, which in turn allowed the agrarian changes to take place without mass starvation and a check to population growth. More than that, however, these economic changes had a profound effect on English society which made it increasingly different from continental. The landlords became real owners of the land instead of feudal lords, and acquired the resources and the motivation to limit the power of the monarchy, enclose the open fields and improve agriculture, sink mines for coal and other minerals, build towns and roads, and encourage industry, overseas trade and empire-building by beneficial legislation or the repeal or non-enforcement of inhibiting laws. English merchants and industrialists, no longer hobbled by gild regulations and internal royal controls, found the whole world open to them, and a strong motive for making their fortunes in the opportunity, rare elsewhere, to buy an estate and join the ruling élite. At the bottom the mass of the population ceased to be peasants married to the land, and became landless wage-earners ready to go wherever work could be found. And at all levels men earned money incomes rather than dues or subsistence in kind, and were ready to spend them as soon as earned, either in investment or on keeping up with the Joneses. With land, capital, labour and consumer demand all geared to economic expansion, is it surprising that Adam Smith found evidence of increasing wealth and prosperity ever since the time of Henry VIII, or that England was the first country to have an Industrial Revolution?[3]

The Industrial Revolution is the *locus classicus* of economic history, for it is here that the modern world, not only in this country but throughout the globe, began. It has pride of place in economic history, since it was undoubtedly the rise of the factory system, of mass production by powered machinery, which allowed both the population and living standards to rise dramatically, created great cities and rapid means of transport, and provided the ships and weapons for European domination of the world and for the terrible wars by which the Western nations disputed it between themselves. The more one looks at the British Industrial Revolution the clearer it becomes that it was more than a merely industrial revolution, that it was also a social revolution which completely transformed the organization of society, a moral revolution which profoundly changed the national character, an intellectual revolution which radically altered men's ideas, and a political revolution which changed the whole basis of central and local government.[4] It is not too much to say that without a knowledge of industrialism and its social consequences it is impossible to understand any other aspect of the history of modern Britain.

The same is true of the history of the modern world, since the leading nations are by definition the major industrial powers. France, Germany, the United States, Russia and Japan have played the leading roles on the world stage because they were the nations which first and most successfully followed Britain's lead. They did so because they recognized—or were forced to recognize—that not merely

wealth and prosperity but political power and military survival depended on industrial strength. Yet, as the less successful industrializing countries have shown, it is not enough
to want to build a modern factory system. It may also be
necessary to change the whole basis and structure of society.
France and Germany abolished feudalism and the gild
system after the French Revolution, and though they did
not do so primarily in order to industrialize it is clear that
they could not have industrialized without. The United
States, an offshoot of British society, had the right kind of
social structure, but even there slavery was an obstacle
where it existed, and the industrializing North determined
to abolish it. Serfdom in Tsarist Russia was recognized to
be the main obstacle to modernization even by the reactionary Nicholas I, and his son Alexander II abolished it after
the Crimean War as part of a general programme of modernization. Even then the emancipation edict of 1861 did not
sufficiently change Russian society to allow industrialization
without enormous pressure on the peasants in the form of
heavy taxation and forced grain deliveries to pay for
capital investment and imports of equipment, and it was
not until the emancipation was completed and the peasants
freed from exploitation by the State after 1906 that the
necessary labour supply and consumer demand came forth
to produce spontaneous, self-generating economic growth
—and by then it was too late to save the Tsarist régime
from revolution. Japan had the swiftest transition from
feudalism to industrialism because she already had a society
which, in spite of a feudal husk, was economically advanced, with large towns, a prosperous coastal trade and a
considerable system of craft production. It was comparatively
easy for the determined revolutionaries who restored the
Emperor Meiji to power in 1868 to abolish feudalism within
ten years and set Japan on the road to 'a rich country and
a strong army', and to get rid of the Western 'barbarians'.

We could go further, and consider what were the social
effects of industrialism in these successful countries, especially
what conflicts between different classes or social groups were
generated by the effort to industrialize, and to what extent

they were able to resolve those conflicts, or to 'export' them in the form of imperialism and foreign war, seeking unity in patriotism and xenophobia. Or we could consider the belated and less successful industrializing nations, and ask how far their tardiness and lack of success have been due to their failure, until very recently, to change their social structures in line with the requirements of modern industry. But we have seen enough to indicate how illuminating and how essential in the modern world is a judicious study of the social and economic history of the major powers. What is true of modern history applies equally to that of any period or area. As will be seen in the chapters on non-European history, especially Latin-American, African and Asian history, the structures of the societies in those less accessible parts of the world are at once so unfamiliar and so vital to an understanding of the political story that their history inevitably becomes a form of general history, and has to start from a basic description and analysis of the society and the economy. It would be no bad thing if all British and European history did the same.

The sources of social and economic history are naturally much wider than those of political history. The political historian, concerned with political leaders and the institutions of government, has the advantage of dealing with the most articulate and public members of society and with those bodies most likely to preserve records of their activity. The letters, memoirs and diaries of the great and famous, the public acts and discussions of kings and assemblies are available to him, though he may find more difficulty when he comes to the grass roots of politics and the identity and motivations of the followers. But the social and economic historian finds his sources as scattered and variegated as his interests. The letters, memoirs and diaries of politicians and aristocratic observers are significant to him in throwing light on life at the directing and controlling levels of society, where ideas, values and attitudes are important because they can more often be put into practice, and where fashions in morals, manners, dress, and almost everything else most often begin; but he is also interested in such personal records at any level of society, perhaps more so as he goes back in time and lower in the social scale, where they become correspondingly rarer. Again, he may be just as much concerned as his political colleague with the public records where they involve social and economic policy and legislation, such as the poor laws or foreign trade, and there are certain classes of public record which concern him far more, notably the statistical returns affording economic or social information, such as customs accounts from which can be estimated the scale and direction of foreign trade; taxation records—subsidy rolls, poll or hearth tax returns, income tax and death duties—from which can be calculated the distribution of wealth and, in pre-Census times, the size and distribution of the population; the Census returns from 1801 with their abundant evidence for every aspect of demographic study and, from 1841 when individual occupations are given, for the social structure of the nation and of every local community; and, from 1838 when civil registration begins, the Registrar-General's annual returns which provide information on a wide range of matters from literacy to the cause of death. The Public Record Office also contains a vast number of royal and monastic estate papers, which make up the world's largest collection of medieval and early modern land, agricultural and village community records.

The records of local government, to be found in the County Record Offices, are also invaluable for the social and economic historian, not merely for local history but as sampling material for regional and national trends. The parish registers are now being used for highly sophisticated purposes by the protagonists of the 'new demography', to yield information about the life cycle of the family, the constitution of pre-industrial households, the stability of the local community and the migration of marriage partners and others between communities, and so on.[5] Poor law overseers' accounts are our chief source until modern times for the state of the lowest section of society. Highway surveyors' accounts give an insight into the state of the roads. At borough and county level corporation and justices'

95

records have much to say on the wide range of matters they deal with, from roads and bridges to crime and riots. Diocesan records contain both religious information—for example, incumbents' returns of communicants, Roman Catholic recusants and Protestant dissenters—and secular information of a surprising richness—for example, the probate inventories which are the best source of what furniture and other possessions most people above the level of the poor left at death.

Private archives are important to the economic and social historian. The records of business firms and of trade unions provide the raw material for two growing branches of the subject, business history and the history of industrial relations. Landed estate papers, now increasingly deposited in County Record Offices, also yield invaluable information on agriculture, mining and other economic activities of landowners, on their relations with their tenants, servants and labourers, on the household consumption of food and other goods and the prices they paid for them, on their social and sporting life, the cost and difficulties of travel, and much else besides. Manuscript letters and diaries are often found amongst them, and are especially useful in putting flesh on the dry bones of household and estate accounts. Best of all, of course, is a visit to the estates and country houses themselves to see the setting in which they lived their lives, the furniture and utensils they used, the gardens they walked in, the fields and woods they farmed and hunted, the landscape they helped to tame and mould. For things are historical records, too, and the English aristocracy and gentry have left more behind them than most other social groups that have existed. But most others have left *something*: cottages and farmhouses, churches and monastic ruins, mills and machinery, town halls and merchants' houses, even parish pumps and urban horse troughs, can all tell us something about life in the past, and the social and economic historian must get out and about and use his eyes for more than reading.

Reading is important, too, as a check and corrective on the mute world of things, and many of the best sources are in print. Newspapers and magazines are amongst the most valuable: it is surprising how the dry minutes of a town council come alive when you read an account of it, abuse and all, in the local press! Economic journalism, of course, has a special use: Sir John Clapham wrote his great *Economic History of Modern Britain* with a complete set of *The Economist* at his elbow. Even fiction, judiciously used, can be revealing. Novels are a well-used source for living and working conditions in the Industrial Revolution, for example, though it is well to check them from non-fictional sources, such as the Government 'blue books' from which so many of them took their information. And the historian has one advantage over the literary critic: bad literature has as much value for him as good, perhaps even more, since the bad novelist or ballad-monger will stay close to what he knows, while the great writer will be more capable of creating his own world and persuading you to accept it.

A special category of printed source is the social survey. One can find precursors of this in Gregory King's *Natural and Political Observations and Conclusions upon the State and Condition of England* (1696) and Patrick Colquhoun's *Treatise on the Wealth, Power and Resources of the British Empire* (1814), but the modern survey has its origins in the Statistical Societies which began in various cities in the 1830s, and made local surveys of poverty and education in Manchester, housing in Bristol, industrial strikes in the Potteries, and much else. It was as a member of the Liverpool and London Statistical Societies that Charles Booth began in the 1880s his famous seventeen-volume survey of London, which was followed up by Rowntree's poverty surveys of York (1899, 1936, 1949) and by the whole great 'survey industry' of the twentieth century. At this point, of course, social history merges with empirical sociology, and in the twentieth century the social historian has the inestimable advantage of working from sources custom-built to supply the answers which for earlier centuries he has to deduce from more esoteric sources.

Enough has been said to indicate the enormous range

and variety of the sources open to the social and economic historian—an *embarras de richesse* indeed. His problem of method is principally one of selection from a vast mass, and to this end he can utilize one or more of a number of techniques. The traditional method may be called 'intuitive induction', by which is meant soaking oneself in the sources until one 'knows in one's bones' what one's chosen society was like and can write about it impressionistically. At its best this can be wonderfully vivid, as in Sir George Young's *Victorian England: Portrait of an Age*. Or one can apply the more usual method of 'empirical induction', used in most textbooks of economic history, with each sector of the economy treated in turn: agriculture, mining, manufacture, internal trade, foreign trade, currency, banking and investment, and so on—much duller but more systematic. 'Sampling', either intuitively—by taking illustrative examples of particular farmers, merchants or industrialists, or representative figures from different social classes—or statistically—by selecting firms, households, incomes, etc., at random and calculating averages, means, standard variations and the like—can reduce the mass of evidence to manageable proportions. Statistics, indeed, are of the essence of social and economic history, are enormously illuminating, and as generally used need not be frightening to anyone with O-level mathematics. Recently a new kind of 'econometric history' has developed, especially in the United States, which applies advanced mathematics to such questions as the economics of slavery or the part played in economic development by railways; but this has been less fruitful and convincing so far than its protagonists have claimed. More useful for the future is likely to be the use of computers to handle, sort and analyse large masses of statistical information on what, electronics and the larger scale apart, is essentially traditional lines, open to anyone who can learn to collect information in a form suitable for punched cards, such as the order number, type and destination of machine tools or the composition of Census households.

Finally, however, it is the use which is made of these

sources and techniques, the end product in actual social and economic histories, which will justify or condemn them, and in the final analysis this kind of history, like all the rest, is an art by which the creative imagination of the historian reconstructs the past in a meaningful pattern. The pattern may be more complex than that of traditional political history, covering more canvas and carrying more detail, but its creation is still a work of imagination which, whatever materials, tools and techniques the artist brings to it, must, like all history, convince by its evocation of the whole life of man in past society, by the persuasion of other historians and the reading public that 'this is what it must have been like'.

SUGGESTED READING

Much the best way to sample the full range and variety of social and economic history is to look at the past and current volumes of the learned journals dealing with the two subjects, notably:

The Economic History Review (published for the Economic History Society by Broadwater Press, Welwyn Garden City).

The Journal of Economic History (published for the Economic History Association by the Graduate School of Business Administration of New York University, U.S.A.).

The International Review of Social History (Royal Van Gorcum, Assen, The Netherlands).

The Journal of Social History (University of California Press, Berkeley and Los Angeles, U.S.A.).

Histoire Sociale/Social History (Carleton University, Ottawa 1, Canada).

Comparative Studies in Society and History (Cambridge University Press).

Bulletin of the Society for the Study of Labour History (Copies from Mr. John Simpson, Department of Scottish History, The University, Edinburgh 8).

Urban History Newsletter (Copies from Dr. H. J. Dyos, Department of Economic History, The University, Leicester).

Agricultural History Review (published by the British Agricultural History Society; copies from Mr. Andrew Jewell, The Museum of English Rural Life, The University, Whiteknight's Park, Reading, Berkshire).

Journal of Transport History (University of Leicester Press).

See also the volumes by various authors in the following series:

Studies in Social History, edited by Harold Perkin (Routledge and Kegan Paul).

HISTORY

The Kingswood Social History Series, edited by H. L. Beales and O. R. McGregor (Heinemann).

Studies in Economic History, edited by M. W. Flinn for the Economic History Society (Macmillan Student paperbacks).

Cambridge Economic History of Europe, edited by M. M. Postan and H. J. Habakkuk (Cambridge University Press, 6 vols. in 7, 1941–67).

CHAPTER NOTES

1. Cf. G. C. Homans, *English Villages of the Thirteenth Century* (Cambridge, Mass., 1941), 'The Frisians in East Anglia', *Economic History Review,* 2nd series, x(1957–58), pp. 189–206, and 'The Explanation of English Regional Differences', *Past and Present*, No. 42, pp. 18–34. For a different, more economic interpretation see, *inter alia,* C. S. Orwin, *The Open Fields* (Oxford University Press, 1938) and Joan Thirsk, *The Agrarian History of England,* IV, *1500–1640* (Cambridge University Press, 1967).

2. H. E. Hallam, *Settlement and Society: a Study of the Early Agrarian History of South Lincolnshire* (Cambridge University Press, 1965).

3. Cf. H. J. Perkin, 'The Social Causes of the British Industrial Revolution', *Transactions of Royal Historical Society*, 5th Series, vol. 18, 1968.

4. Cf. Harold Perkin, *The Origins of Modern English Society, 1780–1880* (1969).

5. Cf. E. A. Wrigley, ed., *Introduction to English Historical Demography* (1966).

100

8

Local and Regional History

John Marshall

The study and writing of English local history is, as Professor Hoskins has recently pointed out, now some four hundred years old. It would be astonishing, therefore, if something of this remarkable tradition of scholarship had failed to find its way into the universities. Its influence is vast, but is often invisible to the naked eye. It is true that there is a very fine Department of English Local History at the University of Leicester, and that other universities have local historians on their staffs. Some, like the universities of Leeds and Lancaster, provide undergraduate courses in local and regional historical study. But the real influence of the subject is far more powerful, far more pervasive, than these facts would seem to indicate.

Looking across the field of higher education generally, one notes that the teacher training colleges produce many hundreds of dissertations annually, many of them dealing with local historical topics. I can say from personal experience that some of these are very good dissertations, and are genuine contributions to knowledge—far more genuine, indeed, in that respect than much local 'history' which reaches published form. Then, scores of graduate students throughout the universities, seeking qualifications in various branches of history or geography, in fact choose local themes for their dissertations and theses. Although, to the best of my knowledge, nobody has yet compiled a full bibliography and handlist of all the resultant mass of apprentice scholarship in local history, there can be no possible doubt that a full survey would produce astonishing results. Purely sectional handlists produced by geographers, or urban historians, covering only a few years of achievement in the universities, make one wonder how it is possible for students of local topics to continue to find themes. Yet the themes are found. For the fact is that this is an enormously rich field of study, a seam of knowledge with apparently endless productive potentiality. Even where two students choose what is apparently the same theme or topic in the same town, there need be no violent or insoluble conflict of interest, for two quite different, but equally good, histories can be written. (I do not say, however, that this type of apparent overcrowding should not be avoided, for the student also derives much joy from feeling that he is occupying untouched territory.)

Each of these hundreds of students, in colleges of education and in universities, shares one vital and basic form of experience with his fellows; he is not only becoming acquainted, often to a high degree of professionalism, with this or that type of historical source, but he is also *finding out for himself*, voyaging into seas of discovery with an occasional radio message from his supervisor or tutor. While the same may be said about almost any thesis or dissertation, whatever its subject-matter—for the lone voyage of discovery is the initiation of the science or arts man alike—it is also a fact that the student of local history is, albeit unconsciously, following the four-hundred-year-old tradition in not only finding out for himself, but also *teaching* himself. For the local history of the past was often written by gentleman amateurs, men following their private interests purely as a matter of love or inclination. This is still largely so today; the private student, the leisure-time worker, the self-taught investigator, still writes most of the local history that is published. (Unfortunately, most theses and dissertations, unlike some very bad local histories, remain unpublished.) This accounts for the enormous variation of standard; the graduate schoolmaster, writing the history of his school or town, may come forward for judgment at the side of a retired businessman who had no formal higher education at all. Some university history departments, only too well aware of the trivial nature of much local history, do not encourage its study as a separate field or discipline. Indeed, the gentleman amateurs of the past, squires and parsons, left behind them another tradition, that of antiquarianism, the collection of facts about objects (monuments, *objets d'art*) or places merely because they relate to that which is old or romantic. In practice this type of pursuit often leads to exacting if sometimes pernickety scholarship, and a firm lack of interest in ideas and movements. It may be felt, with reason, that such attitudes have little place in a university, although one should add that there are many scholars, inside and outside universities, who are both good antiquarians and competent historians, and the diligent, meticulous recording of the antiquary often aids the historian. So, even here, the old tradition is by no means purely negative.

In other respects there have been vast changes in the quality and nature of the local historical material published during the last thirty or so years, especially by county and regional learned societies; it is more interested in problems of social, economic and political history, more directly concerned in solving those problems, far wider in its sympathies, and more resourceful in its scholarship. This may be partly attributed to the universities and to university graduates who seek to use local society transactions to publish the fruits of their research, but also a deepening and enrichment of the subject as more and varied people take an interest in it. And what a fascinating subject it now is!

In the old days, the view of the squire and the parson, when either of these worthies involved himself in writing local history, was a very limited view. The squire wrote about people like himself, and families like his own; important people, it is true, who were leaders of their community, and who did most of the administrative donkey work, but who were still very much a minority group. The parson, more of a scholar, would accumulate multifarious details of church history, and would usually succeed in collecting a great deal of rather disorganized local lore. This would be put between hard boards as the history of a place. There are many thousands of such histories in libraries.

Now, if local history is about anything at all, it is about the histories of given places. But, as has been explained elsewhere in this book, history means a story, a narrative, about the details and changing relationships of men in different circumstances. In the smallest town or village, there are, and were, numerous sorts and conditions of men and women earning their livings in very different ways, and experiencing a great variety of relationships one with the other, marital, familial, religious, occupational, legal, administrative, philanthropic, recreational and so on. Despite the fascinating complexity of these relationships— and if you want to know more about the subject in present-day terms, then read Professor W. M. Williams's *Gosforth: the Sociology of an English Village*—we still habitually and loosely describe the villagers as belonging to a 'community', primarily because they occupy one geographically definable location, with clearly marked administrative boundaries. But there are a great many social groups in or about the village, and the differences between some of them are greater than the similarities; Professor Williams, for example, analyses the habits and affiliations of economic and social classes and sub-classes, from 'upper-upper' to 'lower-lower', and it is plain that these widely differing groups have little in common, although the bulk of the villagers in the middle groups may identify themselves with the 'community' very strongly.

Gosforth, of course, is seen in twentieth-century terms. Let us suppose that we attempt to see any English village or locality, in somewhat similar terms, but *historically*. It is very obvious that the old squire-or-parson type of local history is not going to help us very much, for it tells us very little about the process of change in the English country-side. Nor can we find out very much about the various social groups within the village community at different times. It is also of the greatest importance to know how many people there were in the village or parish at successive periods, if only because an obvious increase or decrease in population may be an indicator of other vital or crucial changes in the life of the local community. A larger population, too, will tend to mean a greater variety of groups, interests and relationships within the major body. However, it is pleasant to be able to record that the interests of hundreds of local historians, inside and outside universities, have now moved towards precisely this type of preoccupation, and this new trend is very much reflected in the work of the Cambridge Group for the History of Population and Social Structure (CAMPOP), which encourages the careful but imaginative analysis of those remarkable records, parish registers, throughout the country.

Given this sort of guidance and stimulus, what questions do local historians now ask? Plainly, if one counts the baptismal or burial entries in the registers one can, subject to certain safeguards, estimate how many people there were in the parish at stated times. But many associated items of information, all to be derived from the same sources, can be equally significant; at what ages did people marry, have children, die? When, and for what reason, did illegitimate children increase in numbers? How big was the typical peasant family, or household? What were the causes of death? Almost immediately, one is deep in problems of social history, for the attitudes of groups of people towards both life and death were profoundly affected by these factors. Here, too, we are concerned with the problems of an entire community and with every aspect of its social structure; one asks how long a labourer could expect to live, how long a gentleman, how long a substantial yeoman. Until a few years ago, these historically important questions were not merely ignored, but appeared almost insoluble. Concerted nation-wide research using common methods of enquiry, the use of standard forms and the employment of a computer now seen likely to produce results which would have hitherto seemed impossible of achievement.

It is true that largely demographic information of this

105

kind can often appear arid, even though the experienced researcher can see much of enormous significance within it. But several other considerations must be borne in mind. Although the demographic work described is the most promising concerted historical research proceeding throughout Britain, the widespread and flourishing study of economic and agrarian history in the universities has meant that an increasing body of background information, touching on the development of given localities, is becoming available. Our activities need not be confined to counting heads, or estimating ages at death; we can now hope to find out something of the agricultural development of the parish or district and the policies of its landlords. We can attempt to relate the study of population movements to the effects of enclosure. And even this is only the beginning. There is religion and the effect of religious movements to be studied, a field stretching far beyond the pile of inert facts about the parish church once collected by the vicar; there is the effect of new industries and changes in agricultural technique and farming; there is the field of riches, possessions, poverty and pauperism; the study of significant local habits and customs—changes in eating habits and diet, for example —as distinct from the merely colourful fictions of yesteryear; and the study of the fortunes of important groups within the community, like the yeomanry.

Words like 'community' and 'group' inevitably recur continually in this discussion, and it will become obvious, too, that some 'communities' or 'groups' have no respect for the administrative boundaries of a parish or a town. They have, or had, a living existence and validity in large tracts of countryside or even in regions. Take, for example, the leading gentry, magistrates and professional people in such an area; they would often, in the seventeenth and eighteenth centuries, refer to it as their 'country', meaning the wider community of gentlefolk to which they felt themselves to belong, over and above the village, manor or estate for which they were directly responsible. Even among the humbler people, family ties extended beyond mere boundaries, and the effect of the latter was weakened still more by the easier travel of the industrial age. Here, then, is one reason for refusing to accept a rigid 'local' in local history. Again, one cannot draw any conclusions about population growth in one parish, or migration, or wages, until one knows something about similar phenomena in other parishes, preferably in the same area or region. For this reason, it is better to study two parishes than one, and twenty rather than two. Despite objections on the part of many amateurs and some professionals in the field, local history does not become less local because the student takes the regional background carefully into account. But it can illuminate national history much more effectively if it samples in breadth whilst examining in depth.

It was pointed out earlier that there is a long tradition of 'teach yourself' in local historical study. Can we now infer that, despite this, the subject is more likely to be taught in universities? This depends upon what one means by 'teaching'. No university teacher stands over his students telling them exactly how to write their essays, or how to read their reference books, or even how to make use of those books. There is certainly a likelihood that more courses will, in the future, be provided for undergraduates and graduates, for the general field now embraces a variety of interlocking disciplines. Similarly, local history is a popular subject with extra-mural classes, and the national body responsible for co-ordinating local historical organizations, the Standing Conference for Local History, now organizes conferences, publishes handbooks and produces an admirable periodical, *The Local Historian.* The university student has the additional advantage of studying history in general, and, if he is lucky, he will have an experienced teacher or supervisor who will discuss his problems and show him the possibilities of the subject he is pursuing. As has been explained, a few universities provide full lecture and seminar courses on local material, and the wealth of published research now available ensures that these have rich and stimulating subject matter. It will be in place to give a few examples, for generalities, although to some extent obligatory, are not really convincing.

It should be explained that the purpose of these examples, and of the type of detailed study indicated, is most emphatically *not* to show that this is ultimate history, the exacting scholar's last word as compared with the superficialities of the textbook and the empty generalizations of the lecture room. On the contrary; however exciting the experience, and however heady and invigorating the air on the frontier of knowledge, the student, if he has wisdom, is far more likely to learn respect for those who have the difficult and dangerous task of generalizing. He will, moreover, find yet another use for his textbooks, and above all, he will learn to use a greater variety of reference books than ever before. The example which follows is based on a long series of learned society articles by a noted scholar, R. C. Jarvis; it is, for a change in the present context, a matter of politicial history; and it deals with a topic which is broadly familiar to every student of British history, the Jacobite invasions.

The reaction of such a student is, at this stage, predictable. Surely this is a national, textbook matter, with most of the important facts known? Quite so; but it is also a local and a regional one, for the Jacobites passed twice, in both directions, through the Cumbrian counties and through Lancashire in their invasion of this country. It will be more to the point to say that the scholarship of Mr Jarvis has made the subject fit into those categories most effectively during the last twenty years or so, by showing how people in those areas reacted to the Scots armies; the county gentry, the militiamen, the parish officers, the religious groupings, even the journalists. To begin at the beginning—why did the Jacobites take that route? The answer is what the textbooks tell us—because the Pretenders, being Catholics, expected support from the numerous Catholics of the north-west and especially of Lancashire, where the old faith had still persisted.

Mr Jarvis, and earlier writers, have had no difficulty in showing that the Jacobite fervour of Lancashire Catholics did not usually give them more strength than was necessary to lift an arm in the toast 'the King over the water'. So, do we give a cynical smile and pass on? Not if we are historians—we ask more questions. If we follow Mr Jarvis, we shall conclude that there is more to the matter than that; the more influential Lancashire Catholics, despite all their disabilities, were becoming assimilated into county society, so much so that their fellow-gentlemen of Protestant persuasion had the greatest distaste for searching their houses for arms. And, indeed, very few gentle Catholics took arms against brother Englishmen; which was very fortunate for the latter, since the state of the militia, the Home Guard or non-professional national defence force of those days, was chaotic and deplorable.

This, too, Mr Jarvis explores in detail. In so doing, he shows us how the country was held together at a time of crisis, by the thinnest of administrative tape. The Lord Lieutenant is in charge of the county militia; but, unfortunately, he is not even in the county when the invasion of its boundaries is imminent. The militiamen hardly have a functioning firearm among them, and, owing to a defect in the law, will in any case disperse after a month whether the enemy is nearby or not. There are, of course, no policemen of the modern type to keep order in the localities, only the petty constables, often local farmers, who have to take their turn at protecting local life, property and conduct. The attitude of the ordinary citizen is, to say the least, ambiguous; the battles of faction and party which fill our more general works of history are plainly not for him. He flies in his thousands at the sight of the Scots army, much to the chagrin of one of the few ardent politicians on the field, the Bishop of Carlisle, who in Whig passion urges the defecting militiamen to sterner resistance, his wig over his eye. His more prudent coachman drives him away, still in that undignified state. Is this not an oblique commentary on the unrepresentative nature of politics in that age?

The less humble had the excuse, when their enemies expected hospitality, of *noblesse oblige;* in both the '15 and the '45, ladies enjoyed the company of Jacobite officers, even if the latter were forgotten when avenging swords or bullets sought them at Preston or Culloden. Somewhat more resistance was shown when the Scots leaders demanded the tax money that Charles Edward decreed was due to him. Collaborationism took a variety of forms, some subtle, some blatant. Meanwhile, the Scots, who in the '45 had the way to London wide open, and who (as Mr Jarvis demonstrates) largely outmanoeuvred the English regular forces, had shown vulnerability in the English body politic. Doubtless the exposure brought its reward in the form of Cumberland's vicious brutality.

All this Mr Jarvis has managed to adumbrate, basing his researches largely on local records. Running through all his published work is a sustained *story,* a developing narrative, the stuff of true history; yet he has also added to our knowledge of military, legal and administrative history. Yet how much more interesting is his material than a dreary recital of administrative and legal functions! We learn not what people were supposed to do, but what they did. On the other hand, a great mass of local historical work deals with more humdrum details of local administration, and it is necessary to read some of this, too, to obtain a sense of proportion.

This, then, is an example of work on the frontier of knowledge, using both local and regional material. There will, in the course of time, be many others, as current examples already show. The impact of political campaigns over large areas, the effect of major movements like Chartism on industrial districts, detailed studies of reactions to events like Peterloo (the subject of recent investigations), all of these studies will both assist insight and add to knowledge. They will not, however, stop further discussion; if the last-mentioned example is anything to go by, they will stoke the fires of political controversy. Other, less controversial topics will also be pursued; the careful analysis of voting patterns and habits in relation to status and occupation (Mr John Vincent's work, as exemplified in his analysis of Victorian poll books, shows how this can be done), the political behaviour of given constituencies, and the development of party politics in local government.

This last example brings us to another developing field

of research, that of the study of urban history, which (like most of the other fields mentioned) has its own organized group of devotees and its own publication. Here, too, the special disciplines of economic, social and demographic history receive full play. The treatment here, like that of rural or agrarian topics, is both local and comparative, and some of the best work now done in the field of local history is performed by urban historians. There are many town histories, but few are really good ones by the most exacting academic standards. One can say, without undue patronage, that the authors are not to blame, for the description of the evolution of a large town is full of the most serious pitfalls and is a work of frightening proportions if it is to be done properly. Yet the sustained study of the development of local communities can point the way to great advances in historical scholarship; as the local historian soon learns, one must not only stand the right distance from one's subject, but also keep it within manageable proportions. One does this by studying communities of manageable size from as many standpoints as possible.

What is the purpose of this? It is to show how a new way of life, an urban way of life, affected groups of people. This, again, can only be done comparatively, but the main comparison in this instance is one through time rather than through space. One studies, first of all, the social relationships of the pre-industrial village, and, later (after examining some side-effects of industrialism on that village), concentrates attention on the relationships within an industrial community or colony of somewhat similar size. Over a long period, the old and the new way of life will co-exist; then, as the urban community grows, and becomes part perhaps of a still larger urban mass, so the new way, the new set of relationships, triumphs. The mill-owner has replaced the rural landlord and squire. Yet there has been no violent change in attitudes on the part of many people; they are still deferential to the new 'squire', the industrialist, especially when the latter is presiding over a still distinct community, but otherwise the new world brings class alignments and conflict. The latter, too, can be studied at close quarters by the local and the social historian, who will not be content with sweeping ideological rationalizations. We must, in all these instances, examine closely the people who participated, and their institutions and their attitudes, thereby learning more about the very fibres of the web of history.

Town history, however, is not an unbroken story of squalor and conflict. Towns are visible growths, the living creations of men, having what is almost the complexity and mystery of the human body. Their institutions are richly various, and range from those concerned with subsistence and labour —trade unions and co-operative societies—to those related to spiritual needs, recreation and sport. There is spendid scope for those who wish to study the history of local theatres and the music hall, or traditional games and customs, and there is a continual open challenge to the future writer of a history of local or regional sport, not as a dreary recitation of games won and lost but as a study of players, spectators and their attitudes. So with all forms of amusement, and with places devoted to amusement; what can be more fascinating than the history of a seaside resort, or, indeed, any kind of resort? The study of the rise of these towns and villages is an important chapter in British social history, one which need not be sentimentalized, but one which is powerfully indicative of the standards and aspirations of the new industrial society—and by no means as dreary as romantics like to think. We can seek the old Adam anywhere, and he looks no more dignified when beastly drunk amid the graves in a sixteenth-century 'church ale'.

Towns and mass activities, of course, cannot be all the story. The splendidly persuasive writings of Professor Hoskins (some of which are recommended below) put a totally different case; local history brings one nearer to the breezes and spring water of the English countryside. Perhaps, at heart, most Englishmen are villagers, and most of us seek rejuvenation, when we can, near to the soil of our forefathers. In recognizing this, we must also face the historical reality of movement and alienation from that soil, or we shall be poorer historians, unable to understand what is happening in other parts of the earth in the present century, and lacking insight into the experiences of those who are once more caught up in great and powerful movements.

SUGGESTED READING

HOSKINS, W. G., *English Local History: The Past and the Future* (Inaugural Lecture at the University of Leicester, University of Leicester Press, 1966).

HOSKINS, W. G., *The Making of the English Landscape* (Hodder and Stoughton, 1955).

MILLWARD, R., *The Making of the English Landscape: Lancashire* (Hodder and Stoughton, 1955).

HOSKINS, W. G., *Local History in England* (Longmans, 1959).

WRIGLEY, E. A. (ed.), *Introduction to English Historical Demography* (Weidenfeld, 1966).

DYOS, H. J. (ed.), *The Study of Urban History* (Arnold, 1968).
  Urban History Newsletter (obtainable from the Department of Economic History, University of Leicester).

READ, DONALD, *Peterloo* (Manchester U.P., 1958).

WALMSLEY, R., *Peterloo: the Case Reopened* (Manchester U.P., 1969).

TEMPLE PATTERSON, R., *Radical Leicester* (Leicester U.P., 1951).

VINCENT, J. R., *The Formation of the Liberal Party, 1857–68* (Constable, 1966).

VINCENT, J. R., *Poll Books: How Victorians Voted* (Cambridge U.P., 1967).

BRIGGS, ASA, *Victorian Cities* (Odhams, 1963).

BRIGGS, ASA (ed.), *Chartist Studies* (Macmillan, 1965).

DYOS, H. J., *Victorian Suburb: a Study of the Growth of Camberwell* (Leicester U.P., 1961).

BARKER, T. C., and HARRIS, J. R., *A Merseyside Town in the Industrial Revolution: St. Helens* (Liverpool U.P., 1954).

MARSHALL, J. D., *Furness and the Industrial Revolution* (Barrow Public Library, 1958).

MARSHALL, J. D. and DAVIES-SHIEL, M., *The Industrial Archaeology of the Lake Counties* (David and Charles, 1969).

ASHMORE, O., *The Industrial Archaeology of Lancashire* (David and Charles, 1969).

The Local Historian (formerly *Amateur Historian*, still published by the National Council of Social Service).

Local Population Studies (published twice yearly in association with Nottingham University Department of Adult Education; obtainable from Tawney House, Matlock).

R. C. Jarvis's work, referred to in the foregoing article, is contained in papers in the *Transactions of the Lancashire and Cheshire Antiquarian Society* from 1944 onward, in the *Transactions of the Cumberland and Westmorland*

Antiquarian Society for the same post-war period, and in a book *The Jacobite Risings of 1715 and 1745* (Cumberland C.C. Record Series, Vol. I, 1954), which deals with the Lake Counties primarily. There are further articles by Mr. Jarvis in the *Bulletin of the John Rylands Library*, and in the *Trans. of the Historic Society of Lancashire and Cheshire.*

9

Modern European History

Clive Church

European history is one of the twin foundations of most
history syllabuses, but its established position does not mean
that it is a traditional or static field of study. Indeed, the
study of modern European history has changed as much as
any other in recent years. It has changed both in status and
in scope. No longer is it the case that European history
is equated with world history or studied because of the prevailing political supremacy of Europe. A few years ago Professor Barraclough and others were arguing that because
of the diminished status of Europe in world affairs there was
no point in studying Europe at all, but this was rather an
extreme view and only partially accepted.[1] Europe is now
studied as a continent in its own right. Its place in British
syllabuses derives from the geographical, cultural and
historical links between Britain and Europe, and not from
any claim to world leadership. In other words Europe is increasingly treated as one continent among several, and
European history has been joined in the university syllabus by both world history in the broad sense of the word,
and by the history of other regions of the world.

Here we are not concerned so much with the status of
European history and its relationship to other parts of the
syllabus, as with the changes which have taken place inside
European historical studies. However, it should be noted
that one of the effects of the changing status of European
history has been to place the colonial expansion of western
Europe in a separate category from the rest of European hist-

115

ory, and as a result this has not been considered here. The first change to note in the study of European history is the trend towards contemporaneity. Increasing attention is given to very recent history at university level, where the terminal date of many courses tends to be later than that in some A-level schemes of study. This is a very understandable development, given the recent political renaissance of Europe, but it is not without its dangers, and here modern history is regarded in a wider sense, as the history of Europe since the sixteenth century. A second change, especially noticeable in some of the newer universities with their schools of European studies, is that European history is seen in much closer relationship to other disciplines, and not as something which is sufficient unto itself. The relationship with other disciplines has taken two forms, one being the increasing use of techniques drawn from disciplines such as the social sciences, and the other being the attempt to relate history to developments in other fields, notably in literature. A similar rapprochement has taken place between British and European history, so that Britain is now seen as an integral part of Europe, and at York is even treated wholly from this point of view.

These tendencies are really a reflection of the third and most basic change, which can be best expressed as the decline of the obsession with power. When Europe was studied as the centre of world affairs, the crucial question was the nature and distribution of political and strategic power in Europe. This interest derived in a large measure from the ideas of the great German historian of the last century, Leopold von Ranke, who conceived of Europe as a unit of six great nations linked together by the mechanism of the balance of power. Since Europe has lost its world primacy the question of power has become of less moment to many historians, who have transferred their attention to the basic characteristics of Europe itself, or in other words to the social and cultural structures of Europe. This change is perhaps more marked at university than at A-level, where a rather desiccated political history in which individuals, parties and states struggle for power in a vacuum, divorced from

116

the cultural and social environment, can still be found. At university one can see both a move to a more rounded political history of Europe, that is, one which pays attention to the background forces—such as the nationalist fervour which gripped Europe before the First World War—and also towards more intensive study of the cultural and social heritage of Europe. It is with this change in emphasis and interest that we are primarily concerned here.

The quiet revolution which has been taking place in European historiography in recent years has served only to add to the considerable attraction of the subject. For those immersed in it, whether professional historians or aspiring undergraduates, it has an appeal far beyond that offered by the history of any single country. Part of its appeal and excitement lies in its sheer difference from the British history with which, as has been recently suggested, we have become surfeited. Because it is less familiar European history has an inherent freshness for many students, and even when one becomes more familiar with Europe there are still sufficient dissimilarities between say the Magyar gentry and the English gentry for the former to retain a patina of difference. Much more than mere difference, however, European history attracts and rewards because of its infinite variety and cultural depth. Within what is, geographically speaking, a relatively small compass, Europe contains an almost bewildering number of states, people, cultures, and institutions, all of which have a long and rich history. This variety, which even today encompasses things as different as the clannish societies of Corsica and Sardinia on the one hand, and the advanced social democracies of Scandinavia on the other, was even greater before the era of mass industrialization and modern communications, so that one is always surprised by the unexpected, the unknown and the different in the course of one's growing acquaintance with European history. Thus although one talks glibly of Italy or the Low Countries one is talking about very different city-states and provinces, the structure and character of which are never quite the same in any two cases. Indeed, there is all the difference in the world between the burgher

117

oligarchies of the provinces of Holland and Zeeland and the rural societies of Groningen and Drenthe. Europe is, of course, not merely a collection of societies, but forms what Duroselle calls a 'superior community', a body to which the different societies feel they belong, and another element of its interest lies in the inter-relationships of the various societies, a good example being the way in which the religious and art forms of the Netherlands spread into England, Germany and France in the fifteenth and sixteenth centuries, colouring the evolution of Protestantism and painting.[2]

Of course, European history is rewarding not only because of its own fascination, but because of its proximity and relationship to Britain. This has often been closer than is sometimes realized today, so that a knowledge of the European past is a useful adjunct to any general education in this country. Similarly, since the development of some parts of Europe, for instance Italy and Bulgaria, has been far closer to that of Asia and Africa than is the relatively fortunate constitutional and economic growth of Britain, the history of Europe can also serve as a bridge to the study of the 'third world'. It is often a parallel, as well as a participant through the process of overseas colonization, to the development of the 'third world'. Moreover, in an era when the future of Europe is under continuous discussion, the study of European history is not without value in offering a cautious corrective to some of the more optimistic and unhistorical rhetoric of present-day European politicians. From a more severely practical point of view, European history also has a great deal to offer for those who intend to make the study of history their chosen profession, since there are probably more opportunities for original research than in some other well-established fields of study.

Not all these facets and developments in European history will have come to the notice of the A-level candidate whose range is inevitably limited both by the demands of the syllabus and by the fact that practically all his or her reading will be in English. At university where more use is made both of monographs in foreign languages and of original sources, the student will encounter them for himself, and will probably discover more in the course of his under-graduate career. This is, of course, also true of other branches of historical study, and it must not be imagined that European history is in a category of its own, with no point of contact with other branches of the discipline. European history obviously has a lot in common with British history in so far as the techniques of investigation of individual national histories are concerned, and with social and economic history in general where the problems of economic backwardness and industrialization are concerned. However, European history does have its own characteristics and challenges, which probably become more apparent at university, and these need some discussion before we move on to a more detailed consideration of some recent developments in the social and cultural history of Europe.

To begin with, the study of Europe differs from the study of Britain or Latin America in that it is not always easy to define. Whereas the boundaries, historically and geographically, of Britain and Latin America are self-evident, those of Europe are not. There is a voluminous and fascinating literature on the meaning and definition of Europe, into which one cannot venture in a short article. Suffice it to say that Europe can fairly be regarded not as a static or geographical entity, but as something that is in a state of continuous creation. Europe is a medley of states and peoples, intermingled in a changing and not always well defined area in the west of the Eurasian land mass, having shared over the last millenium and a half much the same cultural and historical experiences. The old saw 'unity in diversity' thus comes very near the truth, or as Halecki says 'European history is the history of all European nations considered as a whole, as a community clearly distinct from all others.'[3] This rather imprecise definition reminds us that Europe is a community of variation, and in some ways there are several Europes. In social, geographical and cultural terms Europe falls into a number of overlapping regions: Russia and the eastern plains, the Baltic basin, the Balkan peninsula, the Danubian area and central Europe, the

119

Mediterranean littoral, Lotharingia, maritime western Europe and Iberia. The major dividing line probably runs north-south between the Germano-Latin lands of the west and the broader spaces and traditional societies of Slavonic eastern Europe, and these regional differences are one of the essential elements of the European reality. English scholars have been severely criticized for their neglect of eastern Europe, but this tendency is gradually dying away, and universities are paying more attention both to eastern Europe and to a regional approach in general.

Not only is Europe a patchwork of differing areas, but the individual nations of Europe are themselves notable for their own regional diversity, a diversity which often reflects the persistence of independent states until fairly recent times. Thus, to talk of Italy is to talk of areas as different as the industrial north and the semi-feudal Mezzogiorno, whose present situations are partly the result of the very different histories of the Kingdoms of Piedmont and the Two Sicilies. Similarly, to talk of Spain is to combine the two often mutually opposed provinces of Catalonia and Castile, while Czechoslovakia, Belgium, Switzerland and Britain are all nations which comprise several peoples, each with its own language, history and culture. This internal regionalism, and the particularism which derives from it, is one of the distinguishing features of European history, and has often been of acute historical importance. During the revolution of 1831 in Italy for instance, the revolutionaries of Bologna would not combine with those of Modena, even though they were facing the same threat from Austria, because the Modenese were 'foreigners'. Students of French history will also be familiar with the intensely held local loyalties which even at the height of the Revolution of 1789 could cut across political divisions. This internal regionalization makes generalization about Europe doubly difficult, and does enhance the complexity of European history, yet it is in precisely this provincial complexity that much of its charm and attraction, as well as much of its cultural and political dynamic, lies.

Another characteristic of European history which becomes

more apparent at university, is that a view of Europe as a community is hard to obtain at times because of the strength of national interpretations and prejudices. Europe is permeated by the nation-state, and for some authorities this is one of the sources of its historical strengths, just as the existence of competitive city-states in a confined area is held partly to explain the rise of ancient Greece and medieval Italy. Much European history is therefore cast in national terms, in that problems are either considered within the framework of the nation or, more regrettably, from the point of view of nationalist myths. This is not perhaps apparent below university level where Europe is usually seen only through British eyes, but the university Europeanist has to balance the conflicting interpretations of various nations against each other. Historical quarrels have a habit of enduring in historical writings, as the Franco-German friendship treaty of 1963 admitted, and so it is very difficult for example, to obtain a rounded and impartial view of the Habsburg empire, because so much of its history has been written by the subject peoples, who have stressed their own sufferings and struggles under the Habsburgs in order to justify their new-found independence. The stress placed on the role of the nation has also led to a certain 'snobbery of size' which is noticeable at A-level, where Europe seems to consist merely of France, Germany and Russia, with England and Italy making occasional guest appearances on the European stage. This has encouraged the concentration on the great powers and their diplomatic relations, but as has already been suggested, this is less the case today. European historians are increasingly recognizing the existence and achievements of some of the smaller states, which have often been very influential. The rapid industrialization of Belgium, the nationalist upsurge in the Balkans, the pioneering of parliamentary and social democracy in Scandinavia and the initiatives in international justice and co-operation taken by Holland and Switzerland are cases in point.

One of the barriers to coming to terms with the regions and states of Europe is that of languages. Many universities insist that students should have some competence in at least one other language other than their own, for without this they are fated to remain blinkered by the British view of Europe. And increasingly, special facilities are made available for students to improve their knowledge of foreign languages or to learn new ones. One hopes that this trend will increase both amongst schools and universities and that students will use their languages to explore some of the wider reaches of European history that are offered to them at university.

At present then, European history is not merely a matter of six nations and the balance of power, but is a much broader study, conscious of the regional complexity and variety of Europe, cautious about its methodology and bias, and giving more room to lesser states and to structural problems as well as to the narrative of political events. This new European history is studied within much the same framework as other fields of study, although it seems that the survey course bulks larger in European history. The problem of languages and access to original sources tends to limit the number of special subjects and options on European themes, although many universities do offer optional courses on aspects of French and Russian history and special subjects on topics such as the Italian Renaissance, Louis XIV, the Russian Revolution, the origins of the Second World War, and especially the French Revolution. The survey course consists of a narrative treatment of the major nations and themes over a period of two or three hundred years, and is based partly on the need to supply students with background information, and partly on the thesis advanced by Professor Elton (and not universally accepted), that what is long in time is by definition more educative than that which is broad in scope, since it is only over a long period that the basic characteristics of a country can really be appreciated.[4] This approach, which is admirably suited to the history of Britain or America, where there is a homogeneous community with which the student is initially well acquainted and therefore able to appreciate the nuances of change, is less suitable to the more varied and unfamiliar situations of European history. It is therefore not surprising that, in recent years, there has been a tendency both to shorten the periods covered by such courses, and to introduce slightly more analytical and thematic coverage, as with the York course on the Atlantic revolution and the Lancaster courses on European working-class movements and on western European government and society in the sixteenth and seventeenth centuries.

This emphasis upon the major themes of European history has also meant that its study has become more comparative. There is a great deal of research being done in this country on the individual nations of Europe, and one hopes there will be more, since, with the exception of France which for linguistic reasons has been exceptionally favoured, there are many gaps in the study of the European nations, so that in the cases of Poland and Portugal we are virtually reliant on one or two scholars. Moreover, this research is being done increasingly with an eye to the wider horizons of Europe. Sometimes this means putting two or three nations side by side, as with the European nobility in the eighteenth century, or merely illustrating the development of an institution in one country by reference to the vicissitudes of a similar institution in other countries, as Professor Aylmer has done for the civil service of Charles I in England. It can also be a much wider and more scientific form of comparison, treating Europe as a whole or on a regional basis in the manner suggested by Marc Bloch and the French school of social historians who take their name from the journal *Annales (Économies, Sociétés, Civilisations)* which has done much to pioneer the study of Europe on a large scale.[5] Two of the most magisterial examples are those by Braudel on the Mediterranean in the time of Philip II of Spain and by Chaunu on the civilization of seventeenth and early eighteenth-century Europe. Braudel treats the Mediterranean as a geographical and climatic zone and then sets the differing social, economic and cultural structures of the surrounding countries against this, and concludes by analysing the political events of the period as a struggle for supremacy in the Mediterranean between Turks and Christians.[6] Chaunu adopts a slightly more orthodox pattern, beginning with studies of the political organization of the states of Europe, and moves on to consider the changing patterns of supremacy and the reaction of various states to the roles of Spain, France and England.[7] The later phases of the book investigate the social and economic structures of Europe and the intellectual revolution symbolized by the scientific movement and the changing position of religion. Both, however, bring together an immense amount of material, and by fitting it into a comparative framework, succeed in bringing order and meaning to it, casting new light on traditional questions and bringing to the concept of Europe a new meaning and clarity.

This is only one of many new developments in European history, but it is probably the most challenging and stimulating. One cannot hope to introduce students to all of the many new developments in the course of a brief article, and many fascinating things such as the detailed picture of early Sweden, the new light cast on the Polish revolutions of the nineteenth century and the controversies over the Spanish Civil War and the origins of the Second World War must be omitted. What can be done, however, is to introduce some of the most important and interesting debates currently in progress in the fields of cultural, social and political history which, as has already been suggested, are very typical of the changing nature of modern European historiography. It should be noted that a lot of this work has not yet found its way into the text-books, although the series launched by Longmans and Fontana are a splendid exception to this and other generalizations about text-books. Students must follow the book-reviews and debates in periodicals like *Past and Present,* the *Journal of Modern History* and the *Journal of Contemporary History* which, like many of the area studies journals, both British and foreign, give considerable attention to European problems.

One of the essential characteristics of contemporary studies of Europe is the attention paid to cultural life. The recent political discussions on present-day Europe have led to a crop of studies of the idea of Europe, in which the use made of the term has been subjected to a very close examination, in the course of which it has become increasingly apparent that until the seventeenth century the term was used only rarely, and always to denote a geographical entity. Nonetheless, some authorities have suggested that Europe should be defined as a society which has shared in the Graeco-Roman cultural legacy, a legacy in which Christianity plays a large part. There are considerable methodological difficulties in accepting this, but the belief has helped to stimulate some provocative and fascinating studies, one notable example being that by Friedrich Heer.[8] Heer covers the whole of European history but most research has been done on more limited topics, the Italian Renaissance, the Enlightenment, and French and German intellectual society, for example. One period which has received considerable attention is the turn of the nineteenth and twentieth centuries, the so-called *fin de siècle* era in which the easy confidence in the ability of positivist science and the rational individual to solve human problems gave way to what H. S. Hughes calls a 'psychological malaise', replete with forebodings of doom and a belief in the inadequacies of traditional structures.[9] Thinkers like Barrès and d'Annunzio found a new certainty in nationalism, others like Bergson and Freud in the cult of the unconscious, and some like Croce in a new idealism. This period is increasingly regarded as a watershed in modern intellectual history, and the real beginning of the twentieth-century world.

Many authorities have seen in this period the first signs of the intellectual crisis associated with the rise of another topic which has been the centre of much study and discussion in recent years, the fascist movements of the inter-war years. This is an interesting reminder of the fact, often overlooked by A-level candidates, that intellectual concepts and the history of ideas do not operate in a vacuum, but are linked to other historical developments and indeed are often an essential component of social and political history. Thus anti-semitism, which was one of the most powerful ideas of the later nineteenth century, and which, as Norman Cohn has shown, rested in part on the arrant forgery of the *Protocols of the Elders of Zion,* became one of the foundations of the Nazi party.[10] Fascism along with many other European political phenomena is increasingly being treated not as merely the offshoot of the personalities of Hitler, Mussolini and Pilsudski but as a movement which is rooted in the social and political conditions of the nineteen twenties and thirties: the depression, the aftermath of the Great War, the Russian revolution. Research in the massive archives left by fascist parties at the end of the war, which are only now being explored, has pointed to the wide range of countries in which fascism or an analogous movement made its appearance. Finland, Portugal and Eire and most of the countries of eastern Europe all had movements of this kind, as well as the western states more usually associated with fascism. It has also been shown that although individual movements differed in many important ways, depending on the exact political situation and history of the country in question, fascism was very much a European phenomenon. Most movements shared symbols and ideas—the hatred for Marxism and parliamentarianism, the worship of violence and strength, the corporatist ideal which emphasized membership of gilds, trades, industries and professions at the expense of class, and the cult of élites, of race and of the state. The way in which these ideas were expressed and enacted, however, varied greatly from country to country. Thus while in Italy and Germany they were incorporated in a single, hierarchical and semi-military party, in France there was a multiplicity of parties, most of which owed more to the influence of Bonapartism than to that of Mussolini. Similarly, the Falange in Spain was merely adopted by Franco as a convenient tool during the Civil War and was largely dropped when the war ended. In eastern Europe there was an even greater diversity of organization and aims than in the west.

This diversity makes it hard to accept the theory advanced by the leading student of fascism, Ernest Nolte, that fascism was simply a middle-class movement, opposing organized Marxism with its own weapons.[11] Some movements were indeed middle-class, as recent investigation of one small German town has shown, and were directed against the working classes and the parties that represented them, but others were much more diverse in their recruitment, as was the case in many eastern European movements. Moreover, it has recently been shown that in many ways the Third Reich itself was a dual society, embracing both big business and a genuine career open to talents. As with many other problems in European history, reality is not a simple progressive-conservative polarity, but something much more complex, in this case a complicated structure determined by ideology and intra-party struggles. The importance of the struggles between the personal empires and groups inside Nazism has been emphasized in several recent studies of detailed aspects of the Third Reich.

Two of the points which emerge from the study of fascism, that is, the importance of local conditions and the interest in social orientation, can also be seen in another much debated issue, the so-called 'democratic revolution'. The basic thesis advanced by R. R. Palmer is that the French Revolution was not a unique phenomenon which was imitated or imposed throughout Europe, but merely part of a wider movement, drawing on similar social problems, and especially on a shared political vocabulary which began in the seventeen seventies and continued to affect the whole Atlantic world until well into the nineteenth century.[12] This idea has not been too well received in Europe because for Rudé, for instance, it overlooks local variations, but it has prompted both a re-assessment of the revolution and some investigation of its differing impact on areas like Spain and Hungary.[13] In the latter, for instance, the slogans of the revolution were used by the gentry in their struggle with the Habsburgs, and not for the advancement of democracy. It has also been pointed out that even in areas with a social structure similar to that of France, revolution was in the last resort dependent on French arms, and that the course of political events in Europe tended to follow what was happening in France. Similarly, the dangers of equating the *sans-culottes* either with a mere mob or with an industrial working class have been urged very forcibly. They, and movements which partly resembled them such as

127

the radicals in England, emerged from a pre-industrial world of small workshops and shops, and it was this class which carried the revolutionary tradition in England and France, well into the nineteenth century. The social composition of the various revolutionary movements in France and elsewhere can now be much better appreciated because of the large number of very distinguished studies of French society in the eighteenth century which have been published in the last twelve years. They have added a new dimension to our knowledge of the French Revolution.

They have also enabled us to understand a great deal more about the wave of revolutions and risings which troubled mid-seventeenth century Europe. Research on this has two main starting points. One is the idea of a general crisis in European society, advanced by Professor Trevor-Roper, and the other is the re-discovery by a Russian scholar of the wave of peasant risings which plagued France between 1625 and 1670.[14] Trevor-Roper argued that the whole of Europe was troubled by stresses and strains caused by a struggle between court and country factions, while Porchnev claimed that the peasant risings were directed at nobles as well as against royal tax-collectors and therefore represent a class struggle. Neither thesis has gained wholehearted acceptance among Europeanists. Thus, while some people agree that there was a general crisis but advance other theories of its causes and characteristics, others reject it out of hand, a tendency which seems to be gaining strength.[15] The debate has, however, stimulated some very interesting work, particularly on the Thirty Years War—which itself has been re-interpreted as merely part of a longer-term Franco-Spanish struggle. Many authorities feel that the military developments of the war placed an increasing financial burden on states, which was borne by those least able to bear it, while the additional powers which were needed by the states were resented by old-established privileged groups. However, the exact reaction to fiscal and administrative change varied according to local conditions, so that there were great dissimilarities between the Fronde and the Neapolitan rising. Similarly

Porchnev's theories have been rejected in favour of a less schematic and anachronistic suggestion that peasant risings were usually directed against the Crown alone and were often joined by other social groups. However, in order to rebuff Porchnev a great deal of work has had to be done on the peasant risings and on the nature of peasant society, its culture, its psychology and its extreme susceptibility to fluctuations in the harvest, to famine, and to the movement of food prices. In the last few years our knowledge of French society has therefore increased in a startling manner.

It is to be hoped that this will soon be true of other European countries, so that we may get a really detailed knowledge of European society and that the attempt to relate social, political and cultural developments one to another will continue, along with the comparative method. If this does happen, we can look forward to European history being increasingly studied on a thematic basis, with whichever methodological tools are most appropriate, even if these have to come from outside the normal historical approaches. It is also to be hoped that European history will continue to be studied in all periods, so that the equation of European history with contemporary history, which is something of a danger at present, will not become a norm. Such developments will mean that European history will maintain both its place in the university syllabus and its justified claim to be one of the most rewarding and exciting branches of historical study.

SUGGESTED READING

BOWLE, J., *The Unity of European History* (Cape, 1948).

CARSTEN, F., *The Rise of Fascism* (Batsford, 1967).

DAWSON, C., *Understanding Europe* (New York, Sheed and Ward, 1952).

DEHIO, L., *The Precarious Balance* (Chatto and Windus, 1963).

DVORNIK, F., *The Slavs in European History and Civilization* (Rutgers, N. J., Rutgers U.P., 1962).

EAST, W. G., *A Historical Geography of Europe* (5th ed., Methuen, 1966).

LANDES, D. S., *The Unbound Prometheus* (Cambridge U.P., 1969).

RAINERO, R. (ed.), *L'Europe du XIXe et XXe siècles* (Milan/Paris, Marzorati, 6 vols., 1959–63).

STEARNS, R. P., *European Society in Upheaval* (New York, Macmillan, 1967).

129

RUGGIERO, DE G., *The History of European Liberalism* (Boston, Mass., Beacon, 1959).

CHAPTER NOTES

1. G. Barraclough, *History in a Changing World* (Blackwell, 1955), esp. pp. 24–5.

2. J. B. Duroselle, *L'Idée de l'Europe dans l'histoire* (Paris, Denoël, 1965).

3. O. Halecki, *The Limits and Division of European History* (New York, Sheed and Ward, 1950), esp. p. 8.

4. G. R. Elton, 'Second Thoughts on History at the University', *History*, LXIV, 1969, pp. 60–67, esp. p. 61.

5. M. Bloch, *Mélanges Historiques* (Paris, S.E.V.P.E.N., 2 vols., 1963), esp. I, pp. 16–40.

6. F. Braudel, *La Méditerranée et le monde méditerranéen à l'époque de Philippe II* (2nd ed., Paris, Colin, 1967).

7. P. Chaunu, *La Civilisation de l'Europe Classique* (Paris, Arthaud, 1966).

8. F. Heer, *The Intellectual History of Europe* (Weidenfeld and Nicholson, 1966).

9. H. S. Hughes, *Consciousness and Society* (MacGibbon and Kee, 1958).

10. N. Cohn, *Warrant for Genocide* (Eyre and Spottiswoode, 1967).

11. E. Nolte, *The Three Faces of Fascism* (Weidenfeld and Nicolson, 1965).

12. R. R. Palmer, *The Age of Democratic Revolution* (Princeton, P.U.P., 2 vols., 1964).

13. G. Rudé, *Revolutionary Europe* (Fontana, 1964).

14. B. Porchnev, *Les Soulèvements Populaires en France avant la Fronde* (Paris, S.E.V.P.E.N., 1963).

15. J. H. Elliott, 'Revolution and Continuity in Early Modern Europe', *Past and Present*, No. 42, 1969, pp. 35–56.

IO

United States History

Michael Heale

Just over a century ago a Cambridge don resisted a proposal that his university should receive an American scholar every two years to lecture on the history, literature and institutions of the United States, with the comment that 'we shall be favored with a biennial flash of transatlantic darkness'.[1] He had his way and his students were protected from the dark rays of American civilization—but only for a time. Today no British university denies its undergraduates the opportunity to study American culture in some form or other, and certainly American history is now firmly established in this country as a legitimate academic subject. In the last twenty or thirty years in particular, the number of professors and lecturers in American history has increased rapidly in British universities, and while the main phase of this expansion is now probably over, some further growth can be expected.

The extent to which American history is taught in British universities naturally varies from place to place. Virtually all history departments offer general survey courses in United States history, many offer third-year special subjects on a particular period or topic, and some are able to present an impressive range of courses of different kinds. The new universities have generally been favourably inclined towards American history, though some of the older universities cannot be excelled in their commitment to the subject. Perhaps most remarkable is the history department at St. Andrews, which allows undergraduates in modern history to take up to six out of their eight Finals papers in American history, with a ninth on European-American relationships. A few universities have followed the lead of Manchester in establishing American Studies departments, where American civilization is examined as a whole and courses in literature, politics, geography and sociology appear alongside history. In some universities (such as Lancaster), which allow history to be taken in combination with other subjects, American Studies programmes as such do not exist, but by a judicious selection of courses an undergraduate may be able to pursue a scheme of study which contains a substantial American element.

As its rapid spread in British universities in recent years has shown, American history has proved a popular subject with present-day students. The reasons for its appeal are not hard to suggest. Many choose to do it for the same reason that originally attracted several of those now teaching it —for its novelty and freshness. For many students who have thrashed their way through the Tudors and Stuarts and the Industrial Revolution time and again, at O-level and A-level and the first year or two at university, American history comes as an enticing opportunity to do something new. (Although it must be said that these traditional subjects may also provide novelty and excitement as they are pursued to an ever more advanced level.) Some students are entranced by the various manifestations of pop culture, and may take to American history in order to be a little closer to the society with which these phenomena are so strongly identified. Others perhaps harbour the hope that the diligent study of the subject may open up opportunities for free trips to the United States, and although this is a benefit enjoyed only by the few, such visits to American universities, usually accomplished with the aid of travel grants and fellowships, have been described as the modern equivalent of the European Grand Tour undertaken by the young élite of an earlier generation. More prosaically, it seems likely that some undergraduates are led into American history because it enables them to study a foreign culture unencumbered by a foreign language.

Underlying these surface attractions are more serious reasons for studying American history. A nation which can put men on the moon commands attention. Whatever the ethics of modern American foreign policy or of the American space programme, the United States is clearly the most powerful nation in the world to-day and the history of the twentieth century cannot be understood without some knowledge of her role in it. The United States has also had a profound impact on British life in particular. The central place of European history in history degrees in British universities is often justified on the grounds that British culture has over the centuries been greatly shaped by our involvement with Europe, but it could well be argued that in the twentieth century American influences have been the more important. The society and culture in which the contemporary British student has grown up owe a vast amount to the United States, and if he is moved by a concern to know more about his own environment the insights offered by American history are at least as valuable as those offered by European. In a larger dimension, the American contribution to western culture is an immeasurable one, and the student who is curious to know more of the intellectual currents of his time will find his attention drawn irresistibly westwards. All these reasons testify to the 'relevance' of American history, a criterion which modern students tell us is important. Professor Perkin remarks elsewhere on the significance of American history in a world divided between pro- and anti-Americans, and it has been the role played by the United States in international politics, her impact on the domestic histories of individual countries, and her dominating influence on western civilization, which have in large part produced this divided response. The United States is studied both by those who praise her and by those who damn her, for both points of view need to be informed if they are to be credibly articulated.

The strong feelings aroused by the United States may point to a need to know something more about her, but it is not the object of the historian to document partisan attitudes. Most of those professionally engaged in the study of American history would justify their activity simply on the grounds that they find it interesting and exciting. Any student who imagines that the pursuit of history is a sedate and undemanding occupation should read Walter Prescott Webb's 'History as High Adventure', published in the *American Historical Review* in 1959, in which this Texan historian superbly describes his own intellectual battles with the elements. The unremitting exertions of American historians have produced a rich historical literature. Its high standard is in part a result of the excellent and thorough training given to graduate students at many American universities. Sir Denis Brogan revealed recently that he was nearly asked to leave Harvard as a graduate student in the 1920s because of his apparently imperfect command of specific information, a defect, which, as he says, has not been a noticeable characteristic of his later work. One doubts whether any British university would have been so demanding. United States history is, of course, modern history, and like most modernists American historians have been embarrassed by an abundance of source material. Everything that has ever been written about or by Americans is a potential historical source. Manuscript collections have been thoroughly exploited—the papers, letters, diaries, etc., of presidents, ambassadors, editors, businessmen, and prominent and obscure Americans in all walks of life. Even more voluminous are the printed sources—official documents like congressional records and the acts of state legislatures, newspapers and periodicals, published memoirs and diaries, travellers' accounts, contemporary books and pamphlets, and publications of all kinds. And not only written or printed material—historians have also seen significance in paintings, cartoons, buildings and public monuments, even the shape of the landscape. There is nothing that survives from the past, it seems, that the historian cannot turn to his own account.

Perhaps one kind of source which is used more in American history than in most other varieties is the traveller's account. Ever since the first venture in the New World, America has fascinated Europeans. In the nineteenth century in particular British and European citizens visited the United States to observe for themselves the remarkable experiment in democratic government which their American contemporaries were conducting. The most distinguished work to come out of such travels was that of the young French aristocrat, Alexis de Tocqueville, whose *Democracy in America* was a brilliant analytical treatment of its subject. Tocqueville's analysis, while rigorous and perceptive, was perhaps too abstract to be of much use to historians who are concerned with particular day-to-day events, but other travellers left more factual records. The comments and descriptions of European travellers have often been used to embellish American histories, but it must be said that they have seldom been used in a more imaginative way. Edward Pessen's recent essay in *Jacksonian America: Society, Personality, and Politics,* both points up the shortcomings of other historians in the use of this kind of material and shows how it might be better exploited.

But the greater part of modern American historical scholarship is, of course, based primarily and necessarily on more orthodox source materials, and it is almost a truism to say that the greater part of it is conventional in its subject matter and approach. American history is certainly not the poorer because of it. But mention might be made of two styles of historical writing which depart from the norm. First there is what is sometimes known as the 'new history', a kind of history which draws much from the social sciences and which is marked by sophisticated statistical techniques, behavioural models, and a terminology which sometimes pains or intimidates traditional historians. This trend is at its most obvious in economic history, where scholars trained as economists are now competing with scholars trained as historians. Not much interested in conventional historical method, the new economic historians treat history as a science; statistics are their raw materials and quantification their objective: hard figures, their assumption is, can give us more reliable information about the past than letters and diaries. Robert Fogel has written a provocative book about the impact of American railroads on the growth of the nineteenth century economy, arguing from a wealth of figures and a complex technical analysis that the railroad was not the all-important factor in the rapid economic growth of the second half of the century which some scholars have thought. In 1958 two Harvard economists, Alfred H. Conrad and John R. Meyer, published a remarkable article on American slavery. Seeking a new answer to the old question of whether black slavery was profitable, they succeeded in computing the costs of plantation slavery and were able to conclude that the Southern planter received as great a return for his investment in slaves as Northern capitalists did for their investments in industry. Their study precipitated a spate of articles seeking to refute, modify or confirm their analysis, some of which conventionally-trained historians have experienced difficulty in comprehending. But on this issue, at least, some traditional historians have found consolation in the thought that the debate over the profitability of slavery seems to have little relevance to what they regard as the real historical problems, and that, in its almost compulsive preoccupation with figures and abstruse methodology for their own sake, seems almost to be acquiring the antiquarian air that social scientists sometimes attribute to their historical colleagues.

Quantitative techniques have affected political and social as well as economic history. In recent years historical scholarship has been strengthened by a number of analyses of voting behaviour, election returns, congressional voting patterns, the composition of particular social or political groups ('collective biographies'), social mobility, and a variety of other subjects in which it is possible to count heads. The 'new' political historians are usually well-versed in the techniques of the social sciences (though, like social scientists, few would claim to be masters) and their works teem with such terms as 'multi-variate analysis', the 'coefficient of correlation' and the like. But they are well-aware of the need to make themselves intelligible, and have usually succeeded in doing so. The new history has succeeded in revising old interpretations, providing new knowledge, and raising new questions. American history is not, of course,

136

peculiar in drawing on the social sciences, but quantitative techniques have perhaps been exploited more fully by American historians than most others. In part this is a result of the advanced state of the behavioural sciences in America, and in part perhaps a result of the American educational system, in which the undergraduate is made acquainted with a larger number of different disciplines than his British counterpart. Lest the new methods appear intimidating, it should be said that many undergraduates find the new history not only intelligible but they also find in it a freshness and a relevance which the older kind of history sometimes seems to lack.

A second style of history which is to be found in recent American historiography and which seems to depart from the norm is less easy to define, though it is sometimes labelled 'cultural history', in the anthropological sense of culture. By this is meant not the history of literature and the arts, but the history of a people as a whole, embracing all their forms of behaviour, institutions and artefacts. In this sense all history is cultural history, and some American historians have suggested for cultural history the same all-embracing role that Professor Perkin sees for social history.* (This attitude was exemplified at a recent American Studies conference, when the speaker asked if there was an economic historian present and provoked the response from the floor, 'There's no-one here but us cultural historians.') Not all its practitioners would claim this for cultural history, and many of the works in this genre are more modest in scope. Professor David Brion Davis has distinguished three levels of cultural history in recent American scholarship. The first is defined as 'a description of the characteristic styles, motifs and patterns of a given period'; the second moves from the general to the particular, and 'focuses attention on some central problem or antinomy within a culture or segment of culture, such as a literary or religious tradition'; and the third is concerned with the interrelationship between the

* Which, indeed, is the history of society in a similarly anthropological sense —Editor.

137

culture and individual personality.[2] As Davis observes, a particular work may move from one of these levels to another. Several forays have been made into this kind of history by American historians, with varying degrees of success. In practice such works have often been concerned to illuminate the values of a particular past society by analysing its myths and symbols, its fears and aspirations, and the spoken or unspoken assumptions behind the actions of its members. Very influential was Henry Nash Smith's *Virgin Land: The American West as Symbol and Myth,* first published in 1950, which used literary techniques to reveal the manifold and often conflicting visions which the West has held for Americans in the past. Owing much to Smith's inspiration is John William Ward's *Andrew Jackson: Symbol for an Age* (1955), which by analysing what this popular American president meant to his contemporaries, reveals much about the beliefs and values of his era. Another admirer of Smith, Henry F. May, believes that literature and politics are 'the most important and revealing means of American self-expression', and through an examination of their expression in the early twentieth century has sought to portray the disintegration of the old cultural order.[3]

Like quantitative history, this approach to historical writing is not peculiarly American, and, for that matter, also like quantitative history, it is not startlingly new. But works dealing with the beliefs and values, the myths and images, the dreams and abstract conceptions of past Americans have abounded in recent years, and the undergraduate may expect to encounter a few of them. Like quantitative history, too, cultural history has drawn on the ideas and techniques of other disciplines. The influence of anthropology is evident in the very concept of cultural history, as well as in the assumption that something can be learned about a society through a study of its myths. It has also close affinities to literary studies. Some of its practitioners have indeed been professors of English, and others trained as historians have followed them in using novels, poetry and other literary sources as raw material from which to reconstruct the beliefs and attitudes of an age. Insofar as this kind of study is concerned with the life of the mind, it has also affinities to psychology, although psychological theories have as yet been used surprisingly little by American historians (though it might be mentioned in this context that the undergraduate should at least know the meaning of paranoia.) Much of the work in the field of cultural history has been hailed as brilliant, sometimes, one suspects, because the reviewer has not altogether understood it, but it has been relatively poorly integrated into general historical studies. Textbook treatments of, say, the age of Jackson or the Progressive era, while they might mention the contributions of Ward and May, often seem to make little attempt to accommodate their findings and insights in their syntheses of these periods. In part this may arise from unease about the validity of the methods used in such works. There sometimes appears to be a disturbing degree of arbitrariness in the selection of sources supposedly representative of some subject or period, or in the values or concepts assigned to an age. This kind of history undoubtedly requires a fertile imagination on the part of its exponents, many of whom would agree that what they have to offer are hypotheses which they have merely suggested rather than conclusions which they have proved.

But most books and articles published on the history of the United States are concerned primarily neither with quantities nor with symbols. The average undergraduate will spend the greater part of his time reading works of a more orthodox type. There are plenty for him or her to choose from. Probably no other country has had its history scrutinized so minutely. In 1968 alone the *American Historical Review* reviewed over 320 new books in the general field of American history (or closely related areas), and this, of course, does not cover all those published. This massive output is a reflection of the strength of the higher educational system in the United States, with its hundreds of colleges and universities and its thousands of scholars. One consequence of this is a high historiographical revision rate— few topics in American history look quite the same today as they did, say, five years ago. The conscientious scholar

139

may find this rapid revision exhausting, but it is exciting too. The American past, as viewed through the eyes of historians, is always changing, as new ideas and new perspectives are constantly brought to bear on it.

Few historians allow themselves to be disturbed by the multiplicity of works on American history. Their students are provided with an enviable choice in what they read, while they themselves, in their own research, know that there is still a great deal to write about. The American story may be only a few centuries old, but one characteristic of it is its remarkable variety. The United States is a highly heterogeneous country. There is no such animal as the 'typical American'. A Dallas sheriff has little in common with a Harvard professor, a Mid-Western wheat farmer with a Black Power leader, a San Franciscan hippy with a Wall Street banker, but they are all undeniably American. This to many people is one of the great attractions of American history and of contemporary American society—the sheer diversity. In part this heterogeneity results from ecological factors. The United States covers a large geographical area, embracing a variety of geological structures and climatic conditions. The differing environmental influences of the several regions have promoted a number of different cultures or sub-cultures on the American continent. Another reason for diversity lies in the nature of American immigration. The United States is not the only nation of immigrants, but its immigration has been more diverse than that of any other country. Englishmen, Irishmen, Germans, Scandinavians, Italians, Poles, Africans, Jews, Chinese, Puerto Ricans and others have all migrated to the United States in substantial numbers. These different peoples have brought with them their own religions, their own languages, their own ways and customs, their own values and prejudices. They have naturally been slow to relinquish them.

American society, then, is divided along both sectional or regional and ethnocultural lines. This is not to say that there is no uniformity. Enjoying a mass domestic market, American industry has been able to exploit the economies of scale, and standardized products are to be found everywhere. In the twentieth century the mass media—films, radio, television, newpapers, magazines—have fostered a new kind of culture which some have found banal but which may be performing an important unifying function. Political parties, anxious to win the support of as many different groups as possible, have tended to play down divisive issues and to base their appeals in the broadest and most unexceptionable of terms. The national political party has been one of the bonds which has kept this heterogeneous nation together; the empty rhetoric and flexible principles of which the American politician is sometimes accused may be a mark of a canny rather than a mediocre intelligence. The official motto of the United States, *E Pluribus Unum* —out of many, one—though it originally referred to the states rather than the people, could scarcely have been better chosen, and perhaps the greatest accomplishment of the American people has been their success in creating a single nation out of such diverse elements. How this was done is the subject of much American historical writing.

American historians are highly conscious of the complexity of their subject and have recognized the need to dig deeply into state and local history. The student soon finds that he cannot get far by simply studying American history at the 'national' level; the nation is composed of states, and the states of towns and counties, each with its own peculiar character. Many doctoral dissertations now focus on a particular state or city or county. And studies of this kind are not simply exercises in local history; scholars naturally hope that a study of, say, the Jacksonian party in Ohio will reveal something of more than local significance, will cast some light on the nature of the Jacksonian movement generally. Studies of this kind have produced a vast amount of historical knowledge and have sometimes raised new ideas which have had a more general application. But they have also posed a problem for American historians. If a historian wants to write a book describing the Progressive movement of the early twentieth century, what is he to do if a host of local studies show Progressivism to be something different in each state and city? The problems of synthesis

141

are immense, and few historians who attempt to portray the national scene would be foolhardy enough to claim that they have integrated the many regional, state and local studies into the general picture with total success.

But syntheses do emerge and from time to time broad schools of thought may be distinguished. In the twentieth century there have perhaps been three of these, each reflecting the values of the period in which it was formulated. Predominant in the period stretching roughly from the early years of the century to the Second World War were the 'progressive' historians. Often identifying themselves with the Progressives of the 1900s and 1910s and the New Dealers of the 1930s, these historians believed, according to John Higham, that social progress, while desirable, could not be taken for granted and had to be fought for. For them American history was characterized by struggle; they emphasized the importance sometimes of sectional conflict but more often of economic and class conflict in the American past. After the Second World War a new generation of historians reacted against these views, and the 'consensus' school emerged, which tended to minimize the importance of economic and class divisions and to emphasize the continuities in American history. These scholars argued that most Americans shared a common faith; such conflicts as they found they sometimes explained in terms of psychological tensions rather than economic interests. The affluent society of the 1950s and the threat represented by the Cold War perhaps promoted these attempts to find stability in the historical experience, which may in turn explain why some younger scholars in the 1960s, who have witnessed the rediscovery of poverty and the agony of Vietnam, have found the consensus approach inadequate. In the last few years the 'New Left' historians have begun to assault what they consider to be the conservative views of their elders. They have searched for and tried to rehabilitate the radicals of the past, they have viewed with a jaundiced eye the middle-class liberal reformers that the consensus historians wrote about; they have reaffirmed the existence of social conflicts and ideological cleavages in American history.

142

As yet their attacks have made little impact on prevailing historical interpretations, but in view of the large number of radical graduate students now at work in American universities, there seems little doubt that more will be heard from the New Left in future years.

If American historians, like other historians, have viewed the past through the eyes of the present, they also have often been guided by an assumption that there is something which may be loosely called the American character. It is frequently said that much American writing (literary, political, sociological as well as historical) is preoccupied with a search for identity, a perennial quest for an answer to the question posed by Crèvecoeur during the Revolution, 'What then is the American, this new man?' Why Americans have gone dashing off in search of a character, like so many knights in pursuit of the Holy Grail, is a fascinating question in itself, but this quest has perhaps affected historical scholarship in two ways. First, it is the legitimate concern of the historian to examine the ways in which Americans have sought to define themselves in the past. In the nineteenth century, for example, many Americans came to believe that their society was above all a free society, and that it was their destiny to spread the blessings of freedom throughout the world (or, at least, throughout the North American continent). Many fine studies have examined the nineteenth-century sense of mission. Secondly, American historians themselves have not been immune to the impulse to define the American character, to delineate the American dream. Some have looked in delighted wonder at the American experience; in their eyes the nation has lived up to its dream and they have written its history in celebratory style. At the other extreme have been those who have transformed the dream into a nightmare; to them the lofty visions of their forbears have served only to conceal the ugliness and brutality of the real American past. Yet others have stressed the ambiguity and elusiveness of the American experience, and words like 'paradox', 'ambiguity', 'contradiction', sprinkle much of contemporary historical writing.

All this adds fascination to the study of American history.

143

Seen in the perspective of the search for self the individual events of American history take on a greater significance. The Civil War was not simply a sanguinary struggle between two opposing sections, nor immigration a phenomenon which could be measured purely in statistical terms, for both, in some sense, played some part in the effort to define the national character. Each historical event is an act in some larger drama in which the players have sought to determine what it meant to be an American. The historian has thus an invaluable role to play, for if Crèvecoeur's question has an answer, it may be found in a study of the American past.

SUGGESTED READING

BERNSTEIN, BARTON J. (ed.), *Towards a New Past: Dissenting Essays in American History* (Random House, New York, 1967).

DEGLER, CARL N., *Out of Our Past: The Forces That Shaped Modern America* (Harper and Row, New York, 1959).

HIGHAM, JOHN, *History: The Development of Historical Studies in the United States* (Prentice-Hall, Englewood Cliffs, N.J., 1965).

HIGHAM, JOHN (ed.), *The Reconstruction of American History* (Harper and Row, New York, 1962).

HOFSTADTER, RICHARD, *The American Political Tradition* (Jonathan Cape, 1962).

SMITH, HENRY NASH, *Virgin Land: The American West as Symbol and Myth* (Harvard U.P., Cambridge, Mass., 1950).

WOODWARD, C. VANN (ed.), *The Comparative Approach to American History* (Basic Books, New York and London, 1968).

CHAPTER NOTES

1. Howard Temperley, 'American Studies in Britain', *American Quarterly*, XVIII, 1966, p. 259n.

2. David Brion Davis, 'Some Recent Directions in American Cultural History', *American Historical Review*, LXXIII, 1968, pp. 697, 699, 704.

3. Henry F. May, *The End of American Innocence: A Study of the First Years of Our Own Time, 1912–1917* (Jonathan Cape, 1959), p. xi.

I I

Latin American History

Martin Blinkhorn

If, as an earlier contributor, Dr Tuck, has written, the study of medieval history is currently unfashionable in Britain, that of Latin American history has of late become almost voguish. Its pedigree here is a relatively short one. First introduced in two universities in the 1920s as an adjunct to the study of Spanish and Portuguese language and literature, as late as 1948 it was described by the first incumbent of a British chair in Latin American history, Professor Robin Humphreys, as an 'infant intruder' into the nation's history schools. The subject boomed in the United States in the 1950s, but British universities remained largely aloof until in October 1962—symbolically the month of the Cuban missile crisis—the University Grants Committee set up a Committee on Latin American Studies. Its report led to the establishment at five British universities of Centres for Latin American Studies, embracing not only history but also sociology, social anthropology, political science, geography, archaeology and the humanities. In the specific field of history, this initiative heralded a more general expansion so that at the time of writing several history schools offer general and specialized courses in the history of Latin America. Since the teaching of the Centres for Latin American Studies is largely concentrated at the graduate level, this latter development is particularly encouraging for it is from universities other than these that the interested graduates must come.

Notwithstanding this academic progress, to the British in

145

general Latin America is today the darkest of continents. Partly, no doubt as a result of the Imperial connection, the countries of Africa and Asia are more fully reported and hence better known. As 'new nations' they enjoy a novelty value once possessed but long ago lost by the now ageing countries of Latin America. The names of Afro-Asian 'liberators' are still news; those of the Spanish American liberators —Bolívar, San Martín, O'Higgins and the rest—are not only history, but for most Britons history with which they have never come into contact.

It was not always so. In the nineteenth century, British interest in Latin America was enormous. Spanish American revolutionaries flocked to London for refuge, inspiration and support, all of which they received, while British ships and volunteers assisted materially in the colonies' struggles for independence. As English a person as Jeremy Bentham seriously considered emigrating to Mexico or Venezuela, evidence of the widespread optimism felt here regarding the future of the new nations, whilst Canning looked forward to Britain's more or less taking over, if not the control, then at least the commerce of the former Spanish and Portuguese colonies. For much of the century this vision became reality in Brazil, Argentina and Uruguay, which through a system of 'informal empire' provided fruitful outlets for British capital and enterprise. Others displayed interests less materialistic, from the expatriate W. H. Hudson's sensitive and stirring evocations of the Argentinian and Uruguayan *pampa* to Lord Bryce's incomparably perceptive sociopolitical commentary. Even as Bryce wrote in 1910, British economic and political influence in Latin America was giving way to that of the United States. After 1914 British preoccupation with Europe and India drove Latin America from the headlines and ledgers, to which only recently has it begun to return.

Renewed interst is to some extent a symptom of the more general contemporary concern with 'developing' countries, as well as a reflection of the rediscovery by would-be exporters of a lucrative and expanding market long lost. But it is the Cuban revolution, regarded somewhat wryly as a boon by

Latin American specialists in the United States because it brought them a public previously lacking, which has also done most to reawaken Britain to the existence and problems of Latin America. This significant event occurred at a time when the advent of the 'global village' guaranteed it an immediacy of impact absent from earlier, greater revolutions, together with unexpectedly far-reaching political, diplomatic and ideological implications. It was Cuba, not Berlin or Vietnam, which raised the most serious prospect of the Third World War; it is Havana, not Moscow, or even Peking, which has become the cynosure of most youthful revolutionaries. In such circumstances, not even the British can any longer afford to regard Latin America as a distant and unimportant region of which they need know nothing.

Whatever the reasons for the growing interest in Latin America, it is self-evident that in a contracting world, twenty nations with over 250 million inhabitants and the most rapidly increasing population of any region on earth merit serious study, particularly at university level. Although the inter-disciplinary 'area studies' approach may well be the best way of tackling such an examination, this is not to suggest that great benefit is not to be derived from the particular study of Latin American history, the more so since most of its practitioners seek to incorporate the fruits of related disciplines into their own work. At its best the writing and teaching of Latin American history should provide the most satisfactory *integrated* treatment of the area's problems. These are themselves problems of profound importance and a significance not restricted to this particular continent: the effects of the close juxtaposition of vastly different cultures and civilizations; the character and long-term consequences of colonialism; the search of new nations for identity and a workable political system; the impact of population growth, internal and foreign immigration, urbanization and industrialization upon a traditional society; attempts to change society by democratic, authoritarian and revolutionary means. Such themes, though given distinctive —and in the view of the specialist, peculiarly interesting—

colouring by their specific context, are the perennial themes of the historian.

Latin America falls into a unique category as an area of historical study. Whilst it lacks the juridic unity of the United States, with which its position in the Western hemisphere, their common European colonial background, and independence won in roughly the same period nonetheless invite comparison, it does possess a geographical continuity lacking in another possible thematic parallel, the white Commonwealth, as well as a degree of linguistic and even cultural homogeneity not found in Europe. The Iberian colonization shared by the Latin American nations—with the exception of Haiti—brought with it three elements which still serve, despite all disclaimers, to bind together their élites: the related Spanish and Portuguese tongues, the Catholic faith, and a strong cultural Europeanism. Reactions against these phenomena, in the form of anti-clericalism and attempts to promote the art, customs and values of Amerindian civilization, if anything make the underlying unity stand out more clearly.

Whether as the result of perspective lent by distance or, as suggested by the Mexican scholar Daniel Cosío Villegas, for reasons of 'economy', Europeans and North Americans have been far more inclined than the Latin Americans themselves to treat the area as a whole, to risk generalizations and to synthesize. It was a North American historian, H. E. Bolton, who in the 1930s took this tendency to its ultimate conclusion and argued for a 'History of the Americas' incorporating Latin America, the United States, Canada and the West Indies; though few of his countrymen, much less any Latin Americans, were prepared to go so far, it remains true that most satisfactory attempts to synthesize Latin American history, as well as to compare elements within it, such as negro slavery, with their North American counterparts, have emerged from the United States and Europe.

Understandably enough, the Latin American scholar is disposed to place greater emphasis upon the variety and complexity of the region, and especially to single out those features which distinguish his own country from the rest. The student of Latin American history soon learns that in spite of the shared language, religion and cultural values, wide variations in geography, climate and racial composition have resulted in producing not one but several Latin Americas. In southern South America the climate is relatively temperate and the ambiance, in the absence of visible Indian or negroid elements in the population, European; from Mexico through much of Central America and throughout the Andean countries of western South America the survival of a large unintegrated Indian population and the presence of the *mestizo* (mixed-blood) products of miscegenation have created a very different atmosphere and distinct problems; in the Caribbean region and in northern Brazil, the Indian element having largely disappeared has been replaced by the descendants of African slaves and of their unions with whites. Such complexity holds for the historian both fascination and challenge, for while the broad homogeneity of Latin America clearly makes attempted synthesis imperative, the variety below the surface constantly calls into question even the most cautious of generalizations.

Until recent years, Latin American scholars devoted much of their attention to the two main periods of heroic endeavour in their history—the Conquest and the Wars of Independence. To nationalistic writers, depressed by the apparent lack of success of the new nations, these episodes offered drama and concrete achievement, besides satisfying the desire of author and reader for powerful personality and significant happening. Since the Conquest is probably the most fully documented period of Latin American history, most of the facts are known even though their interpretation by native historians differs widely according to their sympathies with conquerors or conquered. The same concern for biography and military exploit formerly characterized Latin American historians' treatment of the Wars of Independence, which viewed in this light appeared as a crucial watershed in the continent's history. Without downgrading the importance or interest of the Independence period, it is probably fair to say that more modern historiography, with its greater attention to the social and economic aspects of the struggle, has led to an increasing stress upon the unity of the century 1750 to 1850, and upon the continuity between the colonial and post-colonial periods.

The student of colonial Spanish and Portuguese America finds himself above all a student not of events but of evolving social, economic and administrative institutions. The importance of these institutions derives not only from the powerful influence which they exerted and continue to exert upon the independent Latin American nations, but also from the light thrown by them upon the broad issue of colonialism in general, the specific relationship between patterns of colonialism in British and Ibero-America, and the currently relevant question of the effects of long-term racial and cultural fusion and adjustment.

Unlike the North American colonists, most of whom arrived from Britain with the intention of personally settling and exploiting relatively small areas of land, the Spanish conquerors and Portuguese pioneers and those who in succeeding generations followed them to America went desirous of acquiring wealth through the exploitation of large estates or mines by Indian or negro labour. Everything favoured the formation of vast estates—the settlers' innate distaste for manual labour, an inexhaustible supply of land and the availability of native and imported manpower. The process whereby the system of large estates evolved was long and complicated, but suffice it to say that by the late eighteenth century the large estate or *hacienda* was the characteristic form of land ownership and use, as well as of rural social organization, in most of the Spanish colonies. Worked by Indian labour attached to it by debt-bondage or peonage, it provided for the need of the owner's family and, at a lower level, those of the peons; in some cases it also produced and exported the primary products required by the mother country. The Brazilian and Caribbean counterpart of the *hacienda* was the plantation worked by slaves imported from West Africa.

When the historian comes to examine the development of Latin American rural society in the century and a half since Independence, he cannot but be impressed by the degree to which its socio-economic infra-structure has survived. In the Wars of Independence, landowners took both sides for a variety of reasons; whatever the wars achieved, they did not bring social revolution. In the upheaval rapid social elevation often rewarded successful low-born military leaders, just as innumerable large estates changed hands. The *hacienda* survived, however, and post-colonial society was dominated by what was, in effect, a *colon* class. In modern terms, the new nations were a string of Rhodesians.

Although the years following Independence brought paper equality before the law and the gradual elimination of the institution of slavery, peonage and indentured labour remained, and the lot of the peon declined as the nineteenth century wore on. Where in the past the *hacienda* had been untypical, as in Argentina, it now advanced; in Mexico, where alone it had been seriously challenged during the wars, the well-meaning but short-sighted reforms of mid-century liberals resulted in its extension and the increased exploitation of the Indians they sought to benefit. As a corollary of the survival and extension of the *hacienda* system, the colonial economy now became a neo-colonial economy. During the colonial era the role of American producers had been to provide the mother country with primary products and to purchase from her manufactured goods. After Independence Spain and Portugal were replaced within this framework by Britain, France and the United States. Legal restrictions no longer existed, it is true, but already the Latin American nations were caught in the web of international trade and investment from which, especially since 1930, they have long been trying to escape.

An important side-effect of the *hacienda* was the failure to develop the type of thriving village and small-town society characteristic of the British colonies; the *hacienda* itself fulfilled most of the village's social and economic functions without stimulating the civic virtues. Cities were another matter, for the first act of the successful Spanish conqueror was almost invariably to found a city. In the British colonies towns grew slowly in response to the requirements of rural communities, whereas in the Spanish colonies the countryside was generally settled from, and in the interests of, the cities. Since wealthy landowners usually preferred, as they still do, to live in the city, and since it was there that administrative, ecclesiastical and cultural affairs were centred, Spanish American civilization soon developed a sophisticated metropolitan flavour unknown in North America, where even in 1800 there were no cities to rival in size or splendour Lima, Havana or Mexico City. During the colonial period and long after, most cities were parasites which governed, distributed and consumed, but did not produce. They were also the centres of friction, for their population included the dominant peninsular Spaniards, ambitious and increasingly resentful creoles (American-born Spaniards) and an inchoate artisan and petty merchant class composed mainly of *mestizos*.

If change in rural Latin America has come but slowly, in the cities it has been profound and its consequences immeasurable. Around 1840 Latin American commerce began to recover from a long post-war depression. From then on, the major cities experienced a growth which is still continuing. In southern South America immigration from Europe was largely responsible; elsewhere urban growth resulted from internal population movement and natural increase, the latter especially since 1930. Seldom was it the result of industrialization, which has never come close to absorbing surplus urban population. Prior to the First World War, Latin American industry represented little more than an extension of the neo-colonial economy already referred to, and it was not until the Depression of the 1930s closed their overseas markets and rendered foreign-made manufactures prohibitively expensive, that leading Latin American nations truly initiated their industrial revolution through state-sponsored heavy industry. Even today there is no Latin American country, save perhaps Mexico, which is not perilously dependent upon the export of one or more primary products—oil, coffee, bananas, copper, tin, wheat, beef and so on.

Historians have been particularly interested in the changes

wrought by urban growth and industrialization upon the
Latin American class structure. Not only have they noted
the formation of a relatively small industrial working class
on the European pattern, but also a much larger 'marginal'
class of unemployed and under-employed poor, often the
most volatile element of urban politics. From around the
turn of the century there is also apparent the emergence of
something recognizable as a middle class, the character,
constitution and political role of which has been and remains
a topic of lively debate among historians, sociologists and
political scientists.

Another such issue is the role and function of race within
Latin American society. During the nineteenth and early
twentieth centuries the conventional Anglo-American picture
of the Spaniards' relationship with the Indian was em-
braced within the so-called 'Black Legend' which portrayed it as fraught with nothing but cruelty and exploitation. Modern reaction against this view has concentrated
upon the role of the much maligned Catholic Church in
protecting and educating the Indian, and the efforts of the
Spanish Crown to ameliorate the lot of its Indian subjects.
Since many of its decrees were never implemented by its less
altruistic servants, such arguments are perhaps themselves
exaggerated, as is the tendency to idealize the happy lot of
the Brazilian negro slave when compared with his North
American counterpart. There is certainly no real question
that by the late eighteenth century, the Indian population
of the Americas was only just beginning to increase after
two and half centuries of decline, that whilst free, land-
owning Indian communities survived the position of most
Indians was one of peonage, and the normal lot of the negro
that of slavery.

The relations of white, Indian and negro in Spanish and
Portuguese America clearly offer parallels and opportunity
for fruitful comparative study with the Indian and negro
policies in the British colonies and, later, the United States.
Any such comparison quickly reveals striking differences.
British settlers normally arrived with wives, rarely inter-
married with Indians or negroes, and if they practised mis-

L

cegenation illicitly, seldom acknowledged or adopted their illegitimate coloured offspring. In the Spanish and Portuguese colonies, nine tenths of the immigrants were men. From the outset intermarriage and illicit miscegenation were both common and accepted, whilst it was normal for the whitest of fathers to treat their *mestizo* and *mulato* progeny, legitimate or illegitimate, as the equals of their white siblings. Whatever the treatment meted out to peons and slaves, inter-racial relationships in the Spanish and Portuguese colonies were less conditioned by prejudice than those in the north. Whiteness certainly accompanied social elevation, but from an early date race-mixing was so commonplace and its consequences so complex that whiteness came to refer less to colour than to status within the colonial caste system. Acknowledged children of whites were 'white' irrespective of colour and as such enjoyed numerous privileges; 'white' status was often purchased by those *mestizos* who overcame the many blocks to their advancement and became prosperous, as well as being granted to Indian chieftains employed by the colonial administrations in their dealings with free Indians. Similarly, the *mestizo* became so identified with urban life that the term has gradually come to mean not only the product of a union between white and Indian, but also an Indian who, having moved to the city, has adopted urban mores and dress; it is thus a cultural rather than a racial term.

By the time of Independence, therefore, although the bottom layers of the social pyramid were entirely occupied by Indians and negroes and, roughly speaking, the middle levels by those of mixed blood, the composition of the élite provided evidence that colour, though a barrier to advancement, was not an insurmountable one. The upheaval of the Wars of Independence made such advancement easier, the revolutionary armies foreshadowing the professionalized armies of more recent times in furnishing opportunity for the rapid promotion of able or ruthless Indians, *mestizos* and even negroes. Many of these quickly aspired to, and several obtained, the presidencies of their nations.

The colonial heritage left an indelible stamp upon the

government and politics of Latin America, just as upon its social and economic structure and its racial composition and attitudes. Colonial administration was almost entirely the preserve of the peninsular Spaniards and Portuguese and within it all authority emanated from the Crown. Apart from ill-preparing the creoles for the exercise of the power which Independence gave them, this system fostered a tradition of personalism and patronage in politics which has died hard.

The new nations which emerged in the 1820s were thus founded upon a much weaker tradition of political participation than their northern forerunner, the United States. The old legitimacy of the monarchy had disappeared, save in Brazil, but no consensus existed regarding the bases of a new legitimacy. The climate of the time and the examples of France and the United States demanded devotion if not to 'democracy', then at least to the principles of constitutionalism. Their realization was rendered improbable, however, not only by the character of the Latin American social structure, but also by the dearth of political culture and an exaggerated emphasis upon military accomplishments resulting from almost two decades of war. While the cultured minority discussed constitutions, almost everywhere effective power passed into the hands of military or quasi-military leaders or *caudillos*. In the absence of agreed juridic and constitutional forms, political disputes of real substance, such as those between clericals and anti-clericals and between the advocates of central and decentralized or 'federal' government, not infrequently brought bloodshed. When this happened the *caudillo* was usually the beneficiary. Poor communications and intense regional rivalries made the task of nation-building difficult; with all their faults it often took the authoritarianism of the *caudillos* to execute it. Although many such leaders were low-born and temperamentally hostile to the land-owning class which continued to wield social power, never did they seriously challenge its grip.

From about the middle of the nineteenth century the hold of the *caudillos* began to slacken as the landowning oligarchy strove to reinforce its socio-economic position through the domination of restricted constitutional governments. In two countries, Brazil and Chile, this stage arrived early, in the former case because the attaining of independence under a representative of the Portuguese monarchy guaranteed continuity. For most of the nineteenth century these countries enjoyed a degree of political stability worthy of the envy of most of contemporary Europe. Other countries, for example Venezuela, did not escape the *caudillo* phase for much longer, but by the First World War oligarchic constitutionalism appeared to be giving way to democracy in Argentina, Chile, Colombia and Uruguay, whilst the upheaval in Mexico promised an outcome perhaps democratic, perhaps authoritarian, but in any event more socially just than the order preceding it.

As subsequent Latin American experience has shown, although the élitist constitutionalism of the late nineteenth century served adequately when the age of mass politics still lay in the future, genuine parliamentary democracy is inevitably a tender plant when, despite the arrival of that age, the old élite clings steadfastly to its privileged position. During the twentieth century most Latin American countries have attempted for lengthy periods to operate a democratic system, but few have succeeded. This is naturally yet another question with which historians are grappling; part of the explanation, at any rate, is that while most of Latin America lacks a sufficient degree of social and economic democracy to ensure the safe working of political democracy, the economically privileged have been unprepared to allow elected governments to carry through the reforms necessary in order that this may come about. They have often been aided by a labour aristocracy reluctant to make sacrifices on behalf of agrarian reform, and until recently by Communists who have seen in the survival of privilege the best hope of successful revolution. In most of Latin America the result of this deadlock has been not revolution but sufficient unrest to imperil the democratic system and provoke military *coups d'état*.

It would be wrong to regard the military, one of the main targets for historical research, as necessarily a conservative force. Until around 1930 this was substantially the case, and if anti-communism is held to be synonymous with conservatism it is still the case today. However, in recent generations the social composition of most of Latin America's previously élitist officer corps has undergone a drastic transformation. Many officers are now of middle- or lower-class origin and are politically and socially radical in a non-ideological and authoritarian sense. Paradoxical as it may seem to Anglo-Saxons schooled in the practices of Westminster and Washington, it is therefore possible that a politically undemocratic military government may offer more to the masses in the way of fundamental social and economic change than an ostensibly democratic system manipulated by the possessors of wealth.

The historian's study of the evolving relationship between Latin American society and politics inevitably leads him to consider whether, since neither democracy nor the traditional type of dictatorship has succeeded in creating a society which is just yet also sufficiently productive to be capable of absorbing the crippling effects of the current population explosion, the answer does not lie in revolution. Modern Latin America has witnessed three: in Mexico from 1910 onwards, in Bolivia from 1952, and in Cuba since 1959. Before 1940 the Mexican Revolution achieved more in the way of agrarian reform than most Latin American countries have yet achieved. Since then Mexico has become a thriving industrial nation, thanks in part to its position adjacent to the United States. Many would argue that the Mexican Revolution is dead, yet if its problems remain unsolved, this is partly because it shares the general agony of seeing increased wealth and production nullified by an even greater increase in population. The Bolivian Revolution, of the same non-ideological character as the Mexican, achieved far less and its direction since the military coup of 1964 is uncertain. Little, however, has been contributed by the activities of guerrillas more picturesque than effective. The Cuban Revolution is still young but has already achieved much, if not in producing wealth then at least in justly distributing it as no other Latin American regime has been able to do. Cuba, however, is not Latin America. Before the revolution it was, in comparison with many of the countries to which its leaders now preach revolution, relatively wealthy, with one of the highest literacy rates and proportions of urban population, as well as one of the lowest birth-rates, in Latin America. It was small, with a population comparatively homogeneous and culturally integrated. The task of Fidel Castro has been and remains difficult enough, but it is as nothing when compared to the problems which would be faced by a would-be Fidel in Peru, much less Brazil.

This necessarily brief discussion has concentrated upon some of the main themes encountered by the student of Latin American history, the aim being to stress the crucial relationship between continuity and change which disciplines other than history are all too inclined to miss, along with the vital inter-relationship of social and political history which those disciplines help to illuminate. There are, of course, other themes barely touched upon—the role of the Catholic Church and Latin America's complex relations with the United States, to name but two of the most important. To most students entering university, the history of Latin America is a totally new field, for there are few British schools into which it has yet penetrated. Perhaps this creates problems not found along more well-worn paths— but it is at least arguable that it is all the more rewarding for that.

SUGGESTED READING

PENDLE, G., *History of Latin America* (Pelican, Revised edition, 1969).
HERRING, H., *History of Latin America* (Knopf, Revised edition, 1969).
PARRY, J., *The Spanish Seaborne Empire* (Hutchinson, 1969).
LAMBERT, JACQUES, *Latin America* (University of California, 1967).
CLISSOLD, STEPHEN, *Latin America: A Brief Cultural History* (Hutchinson, 1965).
MANDER, JOHN, *Static Society: The Paradox of Latin America* (Gollancz, 1969).

12

African and Asian History

John MacKenzie

It may seem incongruous to group together in this way the history of two very different continents, possessing enormous heterogeneity within themselves, and yet it has become quite customary to do so, mainly because Europe and European historiography came into contact with both through the medium of imperialism. Moreover, the writing of history is inevitably coloured by our view of the present, and today much of these two continents is classified together as 'developing nations' or 'the third world', although these terms are already beginning to outlive their usefulness. It is a grouping that has also been institutionalized in various ways, whether in the School of Oriental and African Studies or in the Afro-Asian bloc.

And yet the study of Asian and of African history in Europe began in almost opposite ways. On the one hand scholars were confronted with cultures of great antiquity, richly garnered with ample evidence of past and present grandeur, and above all literate. On the other hand scholars beheld a continent which allegedly had no history, a continent filled with barbarous warring polities where what little culture did exist (using the word culture in their terms) was of alien origin, Middle Eastern or Islamic. Thus Asia provided a respectable field for linguistic and literary scholars, antiquarians, archaeologists and historians. To generations of scholars classically educated, this was an area on which the classical world had impinged, and which could be seen as a logical extension of their classical studies.

159

This was particularly true of India and later of South East Asia where British and French imperialism encouraged such study. In India the study produced a great controversy, historically important in itself, between those orientalists who admired and respected Indian culture and history and the utilitarians like James Mill who sought to create in India a *tabula rasa* on which to imprint utilitarian doctrine. The controversy itself provided an enormous stimulus to the study of South Asian history. In the absence of any of these factors it was not until later that the Far East came into the orbit of the curious orientalist.

By contrast, Africa was scarcely a respectable field for study. Since no literate cultures could be found in most of sub-Saharan Africa, this was hardly a field for the historian at all. The proposition that Africa had no history whatever was an oft-repeated one, and became the principal apologia for late nineteenth-century imperial expansion, though as an apologia it was just as meaningless as the notion that the slave trade was a means of saving black souls. Africa then was to have her history imprinted by her European conquerors, and was fit to be studied only by the new breed of 'armchair anthropologists', using the observations of much publicized explorers and travellers to formulate their racial and cultural theories.

However, mention of 'European conquerors' reflects an important similarity that can be distinguished between the early studies on Africa and Asia. In both cases, the history of the conquerors, Middle Eastern and Islamic, was at once more attractive and more apparently rewarding. As has so often happened in historiography, the conquered tended to be lost beneath the weight of the materials on the conquerors —surely there is no better example of this than Carthage and Rome. And of course Europeans could see themselves in this mainstream of conquest and could become obsessed with their own heroic achievements. The re-discovery of Asian and of African history has therefore been in many cases the re-discovery of the history of the supposedly conquered peoples.

For the curious fact is that explorers, missionaries and

imperial officers, while subscribing to the 'no history' idea, began to exhibit that very curiosity which marks the beginning of all historical enquiry, and which in this case was eventually to break down their basic premise. Where did these people come from? Why does one people predominate over another? What are the relationships between their languages? How did their notions of kingship originate and develop? Questions like these were asked and the answers were sought in the immediately obvious way: ask the people themselves. And the questioners soon discovered that in pre-literate societies memories are much more attuned than in literate to the remembering and passing down from generation to generation of the traditions of the group. Since then quite remarkable consistencies have been found between pieces of oral evidence and documentary evidence from Arabic or Portuguese sources of several centuries ago. Indeed, in some instances it has been demonstrated that oral traditions can be more accurate than written ones.

The European approach to African and Asian history then was born of curiosity, partly of administrative and commercial necessity. There are two good examples of this. When Stamford Raffles set out in 1811 to conquer Java from the Dutch, he took a historian with him in his retinue, for Raffles had already developed a keen interest in the history of indigenous peoples during his period in the settlement of Penang in Malaya. The historian, however, died, and Raffles decided to take upon himself the projected work. The result was his monumental *History of Java,* written largely from oral evidence, written to a great extent out of sheer curiosity, but providing also very practical help for Raffles in deciding on the land settlement he should make in his administration of the island, and the sort of economic development that would make it valuable to the mother country. Unfortunately for Raffles, and perhaps even for the people of Java, his work was completely overturned by the diplomats at Vienna when Java was handed back to the Dutch. But Raffles' *History* remains, and has recently been re-published in a splendidly lavish edition.

Another example is perhaps a somewhat less obvious one.

161

When Europeans and Americans began to trade more exten-
sively on the South China coast in the early nineteenth
century, they imagined that they were dealing with a sovereign
state much like their own, with a foreign office, acknowledged channels of communication with the centre, diplomats capable of making trade agreements, and so on. In
fact of course the situation was very different. China was
called an empire, but this was mere extension of Western
terminology, for there was no machinery for the regulation
of external affairs at the centre. The westerners found
considerable regional autonomy, of a sort, but this did not
mean that they could simply negotiate with regional govern-
ors or viceroys; the latter had no delegated authority, for
the situation had never been envisaged, and simply referred
problems to Peking. And in Peking's eyes the westerners
constituted only the lowest form of life, for such was the
status of traders within China, and more than that they
were regarded as barbarians conducting their lowly occupation on the frontiers of the centre of the universe, the only
truly civilized area of the world, China. The Western consuls
and superintendents of trade on the China coast soon had
a shrewder notion of this situation, as their dispatches to
their foreign offices reveal, than they have often been given
credit for. They were nonetheless determined to impose
European forms on China, but their observations and the
memoirs they published, born of a confused situation they
were required to understand, constituted an important beginning of the study of Chinese society and its history in the
West, even though their concerns were narrower and com-
mercially oriented. As in Africa, it was a process eventually
taken over by the missionaries.

That the creation of an Asian and African historiography
was closely bound up with Europe's grappling with the
wider world and with the efforts of the wider world to
grapple with Europe is amply evidenced by Japan, where,
even during the period when Europeans were held at
more than arm's length, a group of scholars were detailed
to study 'Dutch learning', including the secrets of European
technological and military supremacy, a preoccupation al-

162

ready of some two centuries' standing when Japan began
her extraordinary response to the West in the second half
of the nineteenth century.

The study of the dominant cultures in Asia and of Islamic
influence in Africa began in an orthodox way : study of the
language, the literature and scriptures, the records that are
readily available, the outward manifestations of cultural
traditions in arts and crafts and architecture. But the study
of the less dominant cultures began in such an unorthodox
way as to reveal from the start something of a historiographical revolution. Missionaries and officers in the field soon
realized, even if theorists at home did not, that the idea
that just because a people were non-literate they had no
history, was patent nonsense. Even if the European time-
scale was alien to these peoples, they still had a corpus of
recorded experience transmitted orally, which invariably
went back many centuries. And what was transmitted orally
clearly could only be learned orally. Thus the historiographical revolution triggered off by this early curiosity
was both a conceptual and a methodological one.

It is extraordinary that historians should have become so
obsessed with documents and the written word: ancient
historians, the writers of heroic sagas, medieval chroniclers
were all users of oral evidence; their works are often remembered experience that is written down, sometimes centuries after the event. This is one reason why practitioners
of African and Asian history often feel themselves more
at home with medieval and ancient historians. Another
reason is that medieval and ancient historians seem more
alive to the insights which can be gleaned from the total
study of a culture. And this is absolutely essential to the
Africanist's or Orientalist's trade. It is the hybrid nature
of this study which most disturbs the protagonists of the
autonomy of history as a literary art. It is what makes it
most fascinating for us practitioners.

To be a successful African or Asian historian one must
utilize, or at the very least be aware of, a whole host of disciplines, social anthropology, archaeology, geography, linguistic
analysis, botany, even musicology. Our critics would say

this makes us dabblers, dilettanti. Our friends and we would say that this is but a healthy eclecticism that has itself produced insights for other forms of history.

Perhaps this eclecticism can best be illustrated by a few specific examples from Africa. The problem of the dispersal of peoples, and in particular the Bantu-speaking peoples, in Africa has been illuminated by linguistic analysis, by anthropologists of various sorts operating techniques of highly professional field research, by botanists studying the spread of the yam and the banana from the East, by musicologists examining the spread of musical instruments and a particular kind of musical scale from Indonesia through Madagascar and on into the interior of Africa, and by entomologists studying Africa's insects, which have played such an enormous role in the dispersal of people and of animals.

The misconceptions that grew up around the supposed mystery of the Zimbabwe Ruins, now in Rhodesia, were largely a product of architectural ignorance. Early visitors to Zimbabwe misconstrued its origins partly because they did not exercise their critical architectural faculties sufficiently; they failed to see that its architecture bore no relation to that of the Middle East or North Africa, to which they variously ascribed it, that despite its magnificence its builders were clearly ignorant of the arch, almost even of the straight line; they failed to see its relevance to an African culture, and its connection with more familiar mud and thatch architecture in shape and form. And of course the greatest insights into Zimbabwe and the culture it represents have been supplied by archaeologists and by the ethno-historian using a combination of oral evidence and Portuguese records of the fifteenth and sixteenth centuries.

Another example of fruitful collaboration from my own experience relates to the various settlements which the Portuguese established south of the Zambezi on the high plateau of South Central Africa in the sixteenth century. These settlements had until recently been lost, and little was known about the life led in them or about the indigenous peoples round about. Using Portuguese records it was possible to establish rough geographic locations; a distinguished ethno-historian using oral evidence was able to pin-point their sites to within just a mile or two, and it was then left to the archaeologist to find the surface scatter of sherds of Ming pottery which these people traded (a fascinating connection with the East), and to set his spade into the ground. These rich sites proceeded to reveal not only knowledge of the Portuguese activities in the area to supplement their own records, but also details of the native peoples who lived nearby. And it is the historian who must be the synthesiser in this type of situation.

The role of the artist, the art critic and the art historian has been important too in the re-creation of African and Asian history. There can be little doubt that the outward expressions of Oriental culture in art and architecture that became the material for so many nineteenth-century travel books and the models for the western orientalism symbolized by the Brighton Pavilion provided a considerable stimulus to the study of Asian history. Likewise, it was African art that helped to infuse scholarship with the notion of African history for its own sake and not just as an appendage to European history. Early in this century European artists, particularly those of the post-impressionist French school, began to be fascinated by African art and began to make collections of it. European conquest meant that examples of African art were arriving in increasing numbers in European ethnographic museums and in European shops (a century after the same process for Asia). As the richness of African art was explored, its greatest achievements like the sculptures of Benin, Ife and Nok began to be promoted from their place simply in ethnographic collections to a central place in the whole history of human achievement in art. This had an incalculable effect on the re-assessment of African cultures as a whole.

The study of African history received another stimulus from the growing consciousness of American and West Indian negroes, and their fascination in their origins. African oral traditions, African music, even African languages had never been totally submerged in their plantation environment. Many studies, including those of perhaps the most

165

important nineteenth-century negro writer, Edward Wilmot Blyden, were stimulated by the 'Back to Africa' movements (themselves largely unsuccessful in their primary objective) and the opening of negro colleges in the United States. By the early years of this century these influences had fertilized the studies of indigenous West Africans. By the inter-war years, African music was making its appearance on the world stage through the medium of blues and jazz, thence to enter into the mainstream of western classical music. Curiously enough, Asian music began to exert this sort of influence at a later period.

If this diversity is what makes African and Asian history so attractive to its practitioners, it is also what makes it so suitable for the modern university curriculum, which is much less concerned with the rigid demarcation of subject, and more aware of the value of insights built up from several related disciplines. Hence students of African and Asian history can be helped by the various disciplines enumerated above. Of course they will bring to all these sources the critical training, the capacity to distinguish reliable from unreliable, the ability to assess and corroborate, which are the marks of the historian in any field. Students of the more modern period invariably find themselves more on the threshold of studies like political science, economics, religious studies or linguistics than on the threshold of other historians. In some universities this has been institutionalized into schools of regional inter-disciplinary studies, although this method can sometimes create as many problems as it solves.

Another attraction of African and Asian history is that it involves, or ought to involve, travel for those who proceed to an advanced level. Some historians have been known to discard the necessity of visiting the scene of their studies, but their loss, personal and professional, is enormous. And it invariably shows. My own study of labour migration in South Central Africa has not only involved considerable travel, but has also led into unsuspected wide ramifications. The study became concerned with the migration of Indians, Arabs and Chinese as well as the Africans and Europeans it might be expected to encounter. Of course there are drawbacks too: one has to be able to accept strange climates, unfamiliar food, agonizing journeys, difficulties in communication, even physical danger to life and limb. But in addition to all this one can be a perfectly orthodox historian delving into imperial records in the Public Record Office or the India Office Library, or in the often well-organized, comfortable archives of Africa or Asia.

But it would be wrong to depict African and Asian history as some sort of eclectic joy-ride, as a kind of with-it magical mystery tour. It is necessary now to examine dispassionately the problems involved.

Firstly, of course, the very need for a broad competence creates enormous problems. Very few historians have as yet succeeded in fusing the best products of several disciplines, though many are trying. Even in approaching just the social anthropological material, undoubtedly the most useful, the historian is confronted by an *embarras de richesses*. Detailed local studies have appeared in growing numbers; monumental multi-volume works like the *Ethnographic Survey of Africa* have now been in existence for over twenty years; comparative works like Fortes' and Evans-Pritchard's *African Political Systems* are very useful but unfortunately less common. In approaching this material the historian must have his eyes open to social anthropologists' techniques; he must be aware of their conceptual frameworks, of their jargon, of the theoretical debates that exercise them. In other words he must bring to their work that battery of critical faculties which mark the true historian in the examination of all evidence. If he does so, he can treat social anthropological material as primary source material, since the trusted, genuinely professional anthropological field worker is in direct contact with the principal source, the people themselves.

Of course, a field worker of any description presuming to study a people must have a detailed knowledge of their language, not only for communication, but also because so many beliefs, attitudes, kinship structures and so on are implied within the language and can only be understood through it. There some 2,000 languages in Africa and Asia.

It is obviously outside the capacity of any single human being to encompass such a veritable babel. Here again the historian can rely on the professionalism of the linguist and the social anthropologist. But he must have some knowledge of what goes on in language, how it relates to the total life of people, and he should know at least one language in the area that is his particular concern. With literate Asiatic languages he will encounter the additional problem of a completely different set of characters. At least one advantage of non-literate languages is that they rely on a largely European orthography. Only through the enormous richness, complexity, diversity and euphony of the Bantu languages, for example, can a historian hope to understand that important family of peoples. This effort at understanding is not as recent a development as some might think. The Scots missionary David Clement Scott produced a very fine dictionary of the Chinyanga language of Nyasaland (now Malawi) as early as 1892; he had to create his own orthography for the language, and it was printed on the mission's printing press. Throughout, Scott stresses the magnificent richness and flexibility of the language. This reveals well how missionaries faced with the practical problems of communication could push forward the study of a people by the careful examination of their language.

But there is a much deeper problem than the problem of understanding other disciplines or the problem of language. This is the difficulty of understanding the whole structure of belief of peoples whose world view, whose attitudes towards time and space, the seasons, ancestors, fertility, the land, social relationships, and all the religious ideas secreted in the interstices of this complex system of belief, are very different from our own. To make this leap of comprehension the historian requires both technical skill and enormous, almost intuitive understanding. While the intuitive historical school of Croce and of Collingwood is largely out of fashion now, somehow the Africanist, though wedded to a severe professionalism, understands what they were about.

Another problem in the study of African and Asian history is that a completely new chronological framework has to be created for these areas. Europeans are obsessed with their own time-scale of pre-history (itself a misnomer), ancient history, dark ages, early, high and late middle ages, Renaissance and Reformation, the ages of Discovery, Mercantilism, Enlightenment, Revolution, Imperialism, and so on. Areas of European colonization in North and South America and in Australasia have been able to incorporate themselves into this time-scale, but clearly it is largely irrelevant to Africa or Asia. Here a completely new framework has to be established. It is a problem, but it is also part of the fascination of the study. Various suggestions have been put forward for Africa, and a distinguished Indian historian, K. M. Panikkar, some time ago firmly placed the era of western dominance, which he called 'the Vasco da Gama period' of Asian history, as just a short space of four centuries in the wider context of Asian history in all its great antiquity.

It has been said by Basil Davidson that the discovery of African (and equally of Asian) history by Europeans is comparable to the great geographical discovery which preceded it from the fifteenth century onwards. And one could go on to say that both these discoveries involved the destruction of whole sets of beliefs previously regarded as self-evident. Geographical discovery clearly revolutionized European man's view of the world; and scholarly discovery has no less revolutionized the European's view of himself, of his social organization, and of his artistic values. It was of course a two-way process, although only the non-European revolution was recognized at first.

Now that it is no longer necessary or possible to see the process only in the context of Europe, African and Asian history can be studied for their own sakes and not just as footnotes to European history, as happened during the period of the colonial viewpoint. And yet this is perhaps the principal interest of this area of historiography, that the writing of history has not only provided considerable insights into the time of the people who wrote it—as always happens—but has also played an important part in the development of that history itself. For the creation of this

169

M

study was part of Europe's response to the wider world. Of course, there had been indigenous historiographies, but Europe brought the mass of techniques which began to unveil perhaps more than Europeans bargained for. And, of course, such historical discovery was taken over by the nationalists of Africa and of Asia as a weapon to beat Europeans with, in India from the Hindu Reformation and the creation of Congress; in Africa from the writings of Blyden onwards.

All this reveals that it would be quite wrong to suggest that African and Asian history has only been studied with modern techniques by Europeans. Already some of the most distinguished work has been done by Asians and Africans themselves. By the end of the nineteenth century India was already producing a few historians of some worth. By our period, Indian scholars far outnumber, as is only natural, Europeans and Americans working in the field. Africa too and in particular West Africa has long since produced a school of high reputation. At conferences of Africanists the proportion of Europeans and Americans to Africans themselves changes annually, even though pressing needs for civil servants, politicians, journalists, in the recently independent countries inevitably deplete the ranks of practising historians.

The independence period has been described by one African (Amilcar Cabral) as 'the return of Africans to history' and by another (Tom Mboya) as 'the rediscovery of Africa by Africans'. Both have some grains of truth, but both are exaggerations. However submerged the cultures of conquered peoples became (and this applies equally to Asia), the growing interest and efforts of scholars, and above all the activities of these peoples themselves, saw to it that they never left history. A few peoples have been culturally expunged in human history, but although efforts were made in some areas to do so in the colonial period of African and Asian history, these efforts were quite unsuccessful. Secondly, although Africa may have been rediscovered by Africans (or Asia by Asians) on a continental, even a global, scale, Africans and Asians never forgot their local traditions. They clung to them as a familiar bastion in a rapidly changing

170

world until the social anthropologist, the ethno-historian, the collector of oral evidence could gather these collected memories and begin to piece together—with the help of archaeologists, art historians, and researchers in such related archives as corroborative material could be found—the whole mosaic of pre-colonial Africa and Asia.

There can be little doubt that the rise to independence of much of Africa and Asia has provided an enormous fillip to scholarship in these areas. Those activists who sought to reinvigorate Asia and Africa themselves produced important works, of which Jawaharlal Nehru's *The Discovery of India* and Jomo Kenyatta's *Facing Mount Kenya* are perhaps the most obvious examples. This together with enormous expansion in education began a new quest. But the independence period has of course produced problems too. It has witnessed some areas, geographical and intellectual, cut off, a few archives closed. But the old imperial boundaries remain the principal barrier to research. Often these boundaries do not make sense in terms of pre-colonial history, and on either side of a boundary one is liable to find a completely different political situation, a different official language, a quite different sort of archive, and in some cases no archive at all.

But somehow, despite all these problems, historical scholarship for those areas has continued its remarkably rich and eclectic development, carrying on the traditions of Sir William Jones and his orientalist preoccupations of the eighteenth century, of the Sanskritic scholars, the archaeologists and Egyptologists of the nineteenth century, of Mary Kingsley in her *West African Studies,* an example of a sympathetic European approach, of Samuel Johnson in his *History of the Yoruba,* an example of an early work by an African (both of these dating from the 1890s), of even the politically oriented studies like Dutt's economic histories of India in the early years of this century or Blyden's *Christianity, Islam and the Negro Race,* all of which stimulated debate and research. And this development has in turn revolutionized the whole of historiography, has made historians more aware of the need for catholicity, of the need to study the total life of a people, and has helped everyone to escape the ludicrously restricting view that only literate peoples have a history.

African and Asian history can now be studied at many British universities. There are specialized centres like London, Edinburgh, Leeds, Birmingham, Sussex, but courses can be found in many other universities in combination with more conventional history courses or with political science or economics. In many institutions African and Asian history has continued to be taught only in the context of European imperialism, although this approach is on the decline. African and Asian history can now be seen on a much wider scale, in which European commercial, political, and not least scholarly expansion play but one, though nonetheless a very important, part.

Contrary to popular opinion, the student of African and Asian history finds no paucity of material. The sources are vast and still to a large extent unexplored. Works have been pouring forth since the war, and already the student will find scholarly guides, academic and non-academic, of a distinction equal to those in any other field, to lead him into this rich and rewarding area of historical study.

SUGGESTED READING

PANIKKAR, K. M., *Asia and Western Dominance* (Allen and Unwin, 1959).

THAPAR, ROMILA, and SPEAR, PERCIVAL, *History of India* (Penguin, 2 vols., 1965, 1966).

NEHRU, JAWAHARLAL, *India's Freedom*, speeches, etc. (Allen and Unwin, 1962).

DAVIDSON, BASIL, *Old Africa Rediscovered* (Gollancz, 1959).

DAVIDSON, BASIL, *The African Past* (Penguin, 1966).

OLIVER, ROLAND, and FAGE, J. D., *Short History of Africa* (Penguin, 1962).

LUTHULI, KAUNDA, CHISIZA, MBOYA, NYERERE, *Africa's Freedom*, speeches and essays (Allen and Unwin, 1964).

13

The History of Science

Robert Fox

Scarcely a decade ago it would have seemed quite unreasonable to expect undergraduate historians to follow courses in the history of science. Most historians, it was recognized, had gladly left science behind them at the O-level stage, or even before, and by the time they went on to university the world of formulae, definitions, and experiments that so often failed to work or give the result they should have given was no more than a painful memory which few would care to revive. The choice between C. P. Snow's two cultures had been made and the historian, for better or worse but none the less definitevly, had chosen the culture of literature and humanities. Unhappily the gulf between the scientific culture and the culture (or cultures) of the rest of society still shows all too little sign of diminishing; indeed, the spectacular developments of the last years of our decade— the transplanting of organs and the programme of space exploration culminating in the memorable events of the early hours of 21 July 1969—seem, if anything, to have aggravated the situation by making the scientist appear even more powerful and hence even more alien and remote in the eyes of society at large. Yet it is in this same decade of the 1960s, marked as it has been by a pronounced swing away from science in our sixth forms, that the history of science has at last gained the honourable place in British universities which it has had since the Second World War in the United States and which its champions have long claimed for it here. Now no fewer than seventeen universities in England and Scotland have specialist lecturers in the history of science or technology (compared with only six ten years ago) and courses at the Special Subject level, which call for the detailed study, mainly through primary sources, of a limited period or problem, are available to undergraduate historians at Bradford, Cambridge, Durham, Lancaster, and Oxford. Most of the universities where the history of science is taught also offer more general courses for undergraduates, in both the sciences and the humanities, who do not wish to specialize in the subject, as well as providing facilities for research or advanced study at the graduate level. And the number and range of the courses offered are still growing rapidly.

This recognition of the history of science as a suitable discipline for undergraduate study owes a great deal to recent trends which have affected university education in general. Perhaps the most important of these are the growing flexibility of our degree structure and the move to break down the artificial barriers between disciplines. But this is not the whole story, for the history of science could never have found its way into the curricula of so many of our universities were it not for developments within the subject itself which have served to bring what was once considered as no more than a fitting pursuit for elderly scientists to something approaching maturity as an historical discipline.

The fact that the history of science is now accepted as a perfectly reputable branch of history does not mean, of course, that certain special skills and aptitudes are not called for, in addition to the capacity to handle historical data. Studies of Chinese or Islamic science and of the achievements of medieval Europe obviously demand an intellectual armoury of languages and unfamiliar philosophy which have to be specially acquired, and a glance at Dr Joseph Needham's fascinating *Science and Civilisation in China* (eventually to be completed in seven volumes) and Dr A. C. Crombie's *Robert Grosseteste and the Origins of Experimental Science, 1100-1700* (1953) will show clearly enough how well equipped the armoury needs to be for work at the highest level. Other studies, especially where the recent

174

history of the physical sciences is concerned, call for an understanding of science or mathematics which only a thorough training in a scientific discipline can give. Professor E. T. Whittaker's classic *History of the Theories of Aether and Electricity* (1910), for example, could only have been written by someone with the profound grasp of modern developments which its author, who was professor of mathematics at Edinburgh University, manifestly possessed. And the same point is certainly true of some of the most exciting of current research in the history of science, of which Dr D. T. Whiteside's scholarly editing and interpretation of the published and unpublished papers of Sir Isaac Newton is a particularly good example. However, it cannot be emphasized too strongly that even a knowledge of science, which is most frequently cited as a fundamental requirement for the historian of science, is in reality no more than an auxiliary tool in a study whose basic skills are those of the historian. Like the medievalist's palaeography or the economic historian's understanding of statistics, a background in science is often useful and sometimes indispensable. But for most work in the history of science, whether at the undergraduate or postgraduate level, it is emphatically not essential; in fact, as I shall argue, such a background can even be positively harmful.

Unfortunately the shelves of our school and university libraries bear witness to an age, not long past, when the possession of even the most rudimentary historical skills was not seen as a necessary qualification for the historian of science and when history was regarded by all too many scientists in later life as something that any intelligent person was competent to tackle. The products of this age—the age of the scientist-historian—were in all too many cases examples of Whig history of the very worst kind, mere chronicles of the discoveries and theories which were thought to have led to that true understanding of the workings of the natural world which the authors, especially in the nineteenth century, so often believed they possessed themselves. Most studies which had been discredited, like phrenology, were either ignored or derided, while others, like alchemy and

175

astrology, were treated only in so far as they appeared to have led to advances in what were seen as their modern counterparts (in these cases chemistry and astronomy). The heroes in this type of history were those whose opinions most closely resembled opinions held in the writer's own day; the villains were those who rejected these opinions, regardless of the fact that they usually had good reason to be critical. The revolution in cosmology which took place in the sixteenth and seventeenth centuries provides an excellent illustration here, for the technical inadequacy of their instruments made it quite impossible for either Copernicus in 1543 (the date of his *De revolutionibus orbium coelestium*) or Galileo in the early years of the seventeenth century to *prove* that the earth went round the sun. Indeed, the evidence against the movement of the earth (for example, the unexplained absence of a perpetual wind from east to west and the equally puzzling fact that objects thrown up vertically came down in precisely the same place and not many miles away) was so strong that a certain scepticism with regard to the heliocentric system would have been justified even after Galileo had won the day for the Copernican cause. But the myth which portrays Galileo as the martyr of science and the Catholic Church, which condemned him, as the villain, the unscrupulous suppressor of truth resolved to keep men's minds in bondage, dies hard, and it has unfortunately found its way into literature, even modern literature like Bertold Brecht's play *The Life of Galileo*, which is far from ephemeral.

Not surprisingly this type of history of science has never had much to commend it in the eyes of historians. Characterized, as it so often was, by a preoccupation with the *minutiae* of science and with the futile discussion of priority claims ('Who really discovered oxygen?' was a special favourite), it was patently naive. Much of it was also highly technical, being written not only by scientists but also, so far as one can gather, for scientists. Moreover, and worst of all, it portrayed science as a formidable intellectual pursuit which performed its task of gradually eliminating error amid a rarefied atmosphere of dispassionate debate, detached both

176

from the course of political, economic, social, and general intellectual history (except for the occasional conflict with the forces of darkness, usually identified with the Church) and from the passions, prejudices, and ambitions which ruled the lives of ordinary men. Of course, this view of science as something set apart from normal human activities is grossly inaccurate even when applied to the science of today, for however incomprehensible and remote modern science may have become, it is still subject to political and economic pressures (as in the space race) and to the whole gamut of human foibles (such as those brilliantly, if not impartially, described by Professor James D. Watson in *The Double Helix* (1968), his account of the discovery of the structure of DNA). But 'externalist' influences on the science of the past were even more important, and this is especially true of the period before the nineteenth century, when European science was not yet established as a distinct profession and hence as an activity of no more than marginal concern to the generally educated man. This process of professionalization, which first occurred in France about 1800, then in Germany in the 1820s, and finally in Britain soon after the middle of the nineteenth century, is possibly the most important single landmark in the whole history of science, and it is one which the historian should keep constantly in view. He should see it as highly significant, for example, that it was not until professionalization that the word 'science' began to be used with its modern meaning and to lose its traditional connotation of *scientia* (knowledge in a very general sense, like the German *Wissenschaft*). In Britain the naming of the newly founded British Association for the Advancement of Science in 1831 and the invention, some ten years later, of the completely new word 'scientist' (by the philosopher William Whewell) seem to have been the first signs of this important change.

So whatever science may have come to mean for us today, we may be sure that the study we identify, perhaps all too readily, as science before the early years of the nineteenth century was something very different, so different, in fact, that many historians now see 'science' as a confusing mis-

177

nomer when it is applied to that period. But whether or not we choose to abandon the word science (in favour, perhaps, of 'natural philosophy' or the seventeenth-century term 'natural knowledge'), it is important to bear in mind that the men of the eighteenth century and before who set out to study the natural world did not do so as the members of a profession with clearly defined aims and standards; nor did they do so in search of the sort of truths and theories that we expect the modern scientist to produce. What they hoped to gain from the study of nature was usually something very different, something far less predictable. As Renaissance humanists, for example, they might have arrived at their interest in nature not through any desire to make new discoveries of their own but through a programme of research which led them to study, in a spirit of reverence, all the works of classical antiquity and not merely those of such 'scientific' writers as Archimedes, Ptolemy, and Galen. Or if they were among the seventeenth-century followers of Francis Bacon, they would have seen the understanding of nature as no more than a necessary preliminary to its control and application for the material benefit of mankind. And the same desire for power over nature, though usually for less laudable ends, would have been the motive for anyone working in either alchemy or astrology. Interest in the natural world could also have a religious incentive, and it very frequently did. In the thirteenth century, for instance, Thomas Aquinas studied and criticized the scientific writings of Aristotle not as a scientist but as a theologian seeking to reconcile Aristotelian natural philosophy with Christian belief and thereby to strengthen the faith. Religious conviction also underlay the charitable schemes of Bacon, but it was even more apparent, indeed it was quite central, in the work of such men as Robert Boyle, Joseph Priestley (both zealous Christians who were far more than mere pioneers of chemistry) and those very characteristic Englishmen of the age which separated Newton from Darwin, the natural theologians —John Ray, William Derham, William Paley, William Buckland, and others—who sought to use the evidence obtained in the study of the natural world in order to demonstrate the existence of God. And there were many other incentives as well, ranging from the fashionability of dilettante science in the eighteenth century, which, in 1789, produced that delightful and wholly English masterpiece by Gilbert White, *The Natural History of Selborne*, to the hard economic incentives which, a little earlier in the eighteenth century, caused James Watt to undertake his studies of the physical properties of steam.

In studying the science of the past, therefore, especially in the age before the coming of professionalization, we must expect to encounter an extraordinary diversity of motives, ultimate goals, and underlying philosophies, and although most of these are quite unfamiliar today, we must come resolved to treat them sympathetically. Above all, we must take care that we do not criticize the men of an earlier age simply because their science was not like ours, because they failed to discover oxygen, for example, or the laws of thermodynamics. The making of such discoveries was not their main intention, and it is precisely this difference of attitude to the purpose and scope of science which makes it so difficult for the modern scientist to play the role of part-time historian. It would be idle to pretend, of course, that even the trained historian is without his store of prejudices. But he has a real advantage in not labouring under the dangerous millstone of beliefs about what science is today and what it should have been in the past. Hence for him the medieval scholar wedded to Aristotelian natural philosophy, and the alchemists, astrologers, and natural magicians of the Renaissance do not appear immediately as rather inferior protoscientists whose foolish prejudices constantly led them astray, but rather as men whose activities can probably be made perfectly intelligible and reasonable in terms of the needs and prevailing beliefs of the times in which they lived. Moreover, when it comes to dealing with individuals rather than general movements, he has the advantage of familiarity with some of the complexities and paradoxes of human nature which must be taken into account in studying any historical figure. To him, therefore, it will come as no surprise to find that William Gilbert, long known to the scientist-historian simply as the physician to Queen Elizabeth I who pioneered the experimental study of magnetism, was also—and for perfectly good reasons—an ardent believer in the efficacy of magic. Predictably enough, it is scholars trained in history who have taught us to see Gilbert in this light and who have revealed similar complexities in such men as William Harvey, a convinced Aristotelian as well as the discoverer of the circulation of the blood, and even Newton himself, who, far from being the epitome of the dispassionate, single-minded scientist, was in fact a man whose religious beliefs bordered on the fanatical. And what is even more important is that the historian has also taught us to see Gilbert, Harvey, and Newton not as Janus-faced figures, looking now this way to modern science and now that way to their curious prejudices, but as men whose interest in magic, or Aristotelianism, or religion was an integral part of their science, inseparable from their scientific achievements.

It is with the trained historian, then, that the future of the history of science lies. Clearly there is nothing to prevent the science graduate from gaining his historical training at the postgraduate level, and many of our most distinguished historians of science have come to the subject in this way. But even they would regard their training in history as the source of their basic skills and all would welcome the recent growth of interest in certain non-technical aspects of the history of science, notably in what may be called the social history of science. In this new field Professor R. E. Schofield's scholarly book *The Lunar Society of Birmingham* (1963) is one of the best and most characteristic of the pioneer studies. Since the Lunar Society had as its members several of the most distinguished scientists and industrialists of late eighteenth-century England—including Erasmus Darwin, James Watt, Matthew Boulton, Joseph Priestley, and Josiah Wedgwood—the book naturally contains some discussion of its scientific and technological achievements. But the main purpose of the book—and it is this which distinguishes it sharply from the great majority of other works on the history of science in the eighteenth century—is to place the Society, scientific interests and all, firmly in the context of the social, economic, and even political history of an England undergoing rapid industrial change and hence to study it as a microcosm of the Industrial Revolution with interests extending far beyond science and its applications into the realms of politics and business. It is hardly necessary to point out that such comprehensiveness makes very considerable demands upon the author, but it is encouraging to find historians willing and able to accept the challenge. Another non-technical type of history of science which is enjoying a vogue at the moment is the history of scientific ideas. The justly respected model for work in this field was provided as long ago as 1936 by Professor A. O. Lovejoy's *The Great Chain of Being,* but this has been followed by a tradition of distinguished research, furthered by such men as Ernst Cassirer, E. M. W. Tillyard, and Alexandre Koyré. Many of the products of this tradition have been written by and for scholars and students with a background in philosophy, but most of them also have a great deal to offer to readers, including historians, with no philosophical training. This will be clear enough to anyone who reads Professor Tillyard's delightful little book, *The Elizabethan World Picture* (first published in 1943 but now available as a paperback), which is one of the most brilliant and yet readable of all studies in the history of ideas. In his book Dr Tillyard examines the relevance to Elizabethan literature of contemporary beliefs concerning the physical universe. He shows, in particular, what an appropriate vehicle for the playing out of the human drama was provided by the geocentric universe of Aristotle and Dante, the universe of which the earth was the most degraded part, the place of 'filth and mire' (to quote Montaigne) and in which the degree of perfection and nobility gradually increased with increasing distance from the centre, until true perfection was reached in the abode of God himself beyond the sphere of the fixed stars that marked the limit of the visible world. The style of the book and Dr Tillyard's great reputation as a student of literature have naturally always ensured a loyal following for *The Elizabethan World Picture* in English departments at schools and universities, but it is also a welcome indication of the narrowing of the gap between the history of science and the rest of history that the book is now almost as well known among political and social historians of the Elizabethan period, who see in the prevailing beliefs about the hierarchy of the heavens at least one possible explanation for the acceptance of a hierarchical order as the natural order for society on earth.

Unfortunately for the historian, the re-writing of the history of science as an integral part of history rather than as a remote, technical form of 'kings and queens' history is a lengthy task which has as yet scarcely begun. Certainly as long ago as 1605 Francis Bacon argued that a history of man would be incomplete without a proper account of his scientific achievements, and this view has never since been without its supporters. In the following century Bacon's plea was taken up by men of the stature of Leibniz and Diderot, and in Voltaire's *Siècle de Louis XVI* (1752) and his *Essai sur les moeurs et l'esprit des nations* (1756), both of which gave some consideration to science, it was even partially answered. H. T. Buckle's *Introduction to the History of Civilisation in England* (1857-61), once widely read and admired, did much to further the cause in the nineteenth century and to create the conditions which encouraged Lord Acton, in the last years of the century, to include a chapter on the history of science in his plan for the first *Cambridge Modern History*. But historians who took the history of science seriously were rare even then, and the chapter which eventually did appear in the last volume of Acton's *History* in 1910, written by the Cambridge biologist William Dampier Whetham, was no more than a minor breakthrough, since it was so clearly detached from the rest of the work. Since then the history of science has gradually come to occupy a more central place in our standard histories (see, for example, the contributions of Professors A. R. Hall and D. S. Landes in the fourth and sixth volumes of the recently published *Cambridge Economic History of Europe*). But the fact remains that there are still all too few works like those of Schofield, Lovejoy, and Tillyard, or like Professor Herbert

Butterfield's more general but none the less illuminating *Origins of Modern Science, 1300-1800* (1949), which can be set with conviction before undergraduate historians.

Of course, few teachers of history have either the time or the inclination to wait for an adequate store of secondary sources before venturing into a new field, and this is no bad thing. Indeed, the undergraduates who have decided to specialize in the history of science have discovered, along with their teachers, many of the consolations of the pioneer. In the almost complete absence of guidance from the great historians of the past, and with precious little help even in modern textbooks, they are thrown constantly on their own resources, obliged (where most other historians are simply encouraged) to make their own unaided assessments on the evidence of primary sources alone. The result is sometimes confusion, even despair. But there is much to be said for having the frontiers of knowledge clearly in view all the time, and, at least in the universities of which I have had direct experience, there is no doubt that this compensation far outweighs the disadvantages.

Naturally most of the courses offered to historians are concerned with problems which establish the link with the more traditional forms of history most easily. The Special Subjects at Bradford, Durham, and Oxford, and a number of more general courses in these and other universities achieve this by a study of the scientific revolution of the sixteenth and seventeenth centuries. It is the opinion of Professor Butterfield that this revolution 'outshines everything since the rise of Christianity and reduces the Renaissance and Reformation to the rank of mere episodes, mere intellectual displacements, within the system of medieval Christendom' —which may or may not be true. But it is not necessary to agree entirely with this assessment in order to accept Professor Butterfield's more general point that the scientific revolution should be treated as a major landmark in European history and not as the mere revolution in science which its name implies. For instance, the discrediting of alchemy, astrology, and other magical arts (which was as much a part of the revolution as the more frequently cited rejection of

Aristotelian philosophy) has important implications for social history in so far as it is a possible explanation for the abandonment of witch-hunting activities in the middle of the seventeenth century. Similarly a clear link with political history lies in the fact that many of those who took the Parliamentarian side in the English Civil War are known to have been among the most vigorous critics of the Aristotelian philosophers and among the most ardent admirers of Francis Bacon, so much so that Bacon has even been proposed recently as the philosopher of the English Revolution, the man who fulfilled the role comparable to that of Montesquieu, Voltaire, Diderot, and Rousseau in the French Revolution. And there are many other ways in which the scientific revolution made its mark on general history, most notably perhaps in the work of those philosophers of the eighteenth-century Enlightenment, such as Hume and Montesquieu, who sought to apply scientific principles in their studies of man and society. An equally rich and illuminating field for the historian lies in the revolution in biological thought which followed the publication of Charles Darwin's *Origin of Species* in 1859, and this is now studied in the Special Subjects offered at Cambridge and Lancaster. Here the emphasis is not on the technicalities of Darwin's theory of evolution by natural selection but on the changes which the theory brought about in the generally educated man's view of his own place in the creation. Once such a man accepted that the race to which he belonged had not been specially created, Genesis-fashion, as the culmination of a grand design but had emerged almost by chance as the end-product of an evolutionary process of incredible duration, God's role became in his eyes that of a remote prime mover rather than that of an ever-present deity. The rejection of the natural theology of Paley, which had become standard doctrine, at least in Anglican circles, by the middle of the nineteenth century, was only one of the many changes which resulted in the field of religious thought. Theories affecting society similarly came in for revision. The champions of the nineteenth-century doctrine of progress found 'scientific' support for their beliefs in Darwin's description of species

184

gradually adapting themselves over the aeons of time so as to become fitter for the task of survival. Marx and Engels saw the evolutionary struggle as the counterpart of the class war, and Marx was so enamoured of this idea that he even sought permission to dedicate the English edition of *Das Kapital* to Darwin (though Darwin, who was suspicious of any attempt to apply his theory outside the realm of science, firmly refused). Evolution could also be used to buttress racial doctrines, although it is an indication of the complexity of the problems awaiting the historian that subtleties of interpretation allowed Darwin to be invoked, on the one hand, by Hitler and the supporters of slavery in nineteenth-century America and, on the other, by those who opposed them most bitterly on the racial question. Evolution, in other words, could be made to show the individuality of the various races or it could be used as evidence of their common ancestry.

Although this is a book addressed primarily to intending students of history, it would be wrong to conclude without some further reference to the courses in the history of science which are offered at many of our universities to undergraduate scientists and technologists. These are usually studied either as one of the three or four first-year subjects which most scientists are obliged to read or as a minor subject in the second or third years of the degree course, although at Cambridge the whole of Part II in the Natural Sciences Tripos (a one-year course) may now be spent in reading the history and philosophy of science, while Leeds offers a joint degree in the history and philosophy of science combined with one of the traditional science subjects. Clearly the scientist's requirements are very different from those of the undergraduate historian. He is normally studying the history of science not as an end in itself (except perhaps at Cambridge and Leeds) nor in order to illuminate some other branch of history, but rather as a means of deepening his understanding of science. He will be particularly interested to investigate the problems which confronted the men who formulated concepts, like force and entropy, which, although in daily use, are often so imperfectly understood by the scientist. And he will be encouraged to examine afresh

185

N

(or possibly for the first time) the evidence for beliefs, such as the atomic theory of matter, which he has come to accept almost as God-given truths. But even though his aim is to become a more critical and hence a better scientist, he must approach the history of science as an historical discipline and be prepared to learn at least something of the historian's craft.

If he is willing and able to do this, he will find in the history of science a study which offers intellectual challenge, extraordinary diversity, and, most important of all, the delights which are familiar enough to any student of history.

SUGGESTED READING

BURROW, J. W., *Evolution and Society* (Cambridge University Press, 1966).

BUTTERFIELD, H., *The Origins of Modern Science, 1300–1800* (new edition, Bell, 1957).

GILLISPIE, C. C., *Genesis and Geology* (Harvard University Press, 1951; Harper paperback, 1959).

HILL, C., *Intellectual Origins of the English Revolution* (The Clarendon Press, 1965).

KUHN, T. S., *The Structure of Scientific Revolutions* (Chicago University Press, 1962; Chicago University Press paperback, 1964).

LOVEJOY, A. O., *The Great Chain of Being* (Harvard University Press, 1936; Harper paperback, 1960).

SCHOFIELD, R. E., *The Lunar Society of Birmingham* (The Clarendon Press, 1963).

TILLYARD, E. M. W., *The Elizabethan World Picture* (Chatto & Windus, 1943; Peregrine paperback, 1963).

Appendix I

The following tables are intended as a brief introductory
guide to the full range of opportunities for the study of
history at degree level. They are therefore not comprehensive
and in all cases prospective students should seek more detailed information from the institutions of their choice and
from the many guides to university entrance and associated
topics. Thus for information about entrance the following
books may be consulted:

How to Apply for Admission to a University (from
U.C.C.A., P.O. Box 28, Cheltenham, Gloucs., GL50 IHY,
June 1970 and annually).

*A Compendium of University Entrance Requirements for
First Degree Courses in the United Kingdom 1970-1,*
London (Association of Commonwealth Universities,
September 1970 and annually).

For an analysis of various degree schemes the student can
turn to a variety of publications, especially

Careers Research and Advisory Centre, *Degree Course
Guide 1969-70: History* (Cambridge, 1969).

G. Barlow, *History at the Universities* (Historical Association, 2nd ed., 1968).

The last mentioned work has given rise to three interesting
articles which survey and assess the range of historical studies
in the United Kingdom. These are 'History at the Universities, 1968: a Commentary' by Brian Harrison, who describes
the opportunities available, 'Second Thoughts on History

187

at the Universities' by G. R. Elton, who takes issue with some modern trends, and 'History at the Universities: Change without decay' by A. G. Hopkins, who attempts to answer some of Elton's criticisms, and appear in *History*, October 1968, February 1969, and October 1969, Nos. 179 (pp. 357-80), 180 (pp. 60-7), and 182 (pp. 331-7). See also R. A. Buchanan, 'History at the Technological Universities', *Universities Quarterly*, Winter 1969, vol. 24, no. 1. (pp. 60-7).

It should also be noted that opportunites for studying history at first degree level are available in some Polytechnics and Colleges of Technology, either through the external degree schemes of London University (External Registrar, Senate House, Malet Street, London W.C.1) or through schemes authorized by the Council for National Academic Awards (3, Devonshire Street, London, WIN 2BA). There is plenty of literature available on these, for instance

Compendium of Degree Courses, 1969 (C.N.A.A. 1969).

A Compendium of Advanced Courses in Technical Colleges 1969-70 (The Regional Advisory Councils, Tavistock House South, Tavistock Square, London, W.C.1., 1969).

The Directory of Further Education (Cornmarket Press, 1968).

A list of such Colleges is given in Appendix I, Table 3, pp. 194-5.

NOTES TO TABLES

Table 1A: Entry Requirements
This excludes general university entrance requirements and covers simply the additional qualifications demanded or recommended for the honours degree or the nearest equivalent. Combined and other degrees have only been touched on in certain instances, signified by :

  e = requirement for schemes involving economic history, etc.;

  m = a scheme involving mediaeval or ancient history, and

  c = a comparative and modern language oriented course.

188

Other Symbols

O = an Ordinary level requirement.

A = an Advanced level requirement.

R = a reading knowledge of a language recommended which can be found in some instances where no formal qualifications are asked for).

Table IB: Degree Schemes

This attempts to indicate the range of degree schemes in which history is an important element. It deals only with schemes which lead directly to a degree and not with Part I or introductory courses which can often be of a different nature from the final degree scheme; nor does it claim to be fully comprehensive.

The following are the definitions of the various categories of degree schemes used in the table :

Single Honours = a degree entirely composed of history, whether ancient, medieval, or modern, or all three.

Combined = schemes in which history is studied on a parallel basis with another subject, a social science (e.g. politics, economics, law, psychology, etc.), a modern foreign language, another arts subject (e.g. English, philosophy, theology, classics, etc.) or a subject which does not fit into any of these categories (e.g. Geography, Education, Science).

Pass = a degree of lower standing than the above, in which history is one of three or four subjects studied independently.

Integrated = a scheme of study again involving several subjects, but which is of honours standing and where subjects are studied in relation to one another. Such courses are mainly found in New Universities.

Area Studies = courses in the total civilization of a country or region, in which history figures to a varying extent.

Other = other schemes in which history figures, normally a specialized course in a topic like Mediaeval Studies.

Econ. Hist. Honours and *Econ. Hist. Combined* = as under Single Honours and Combined but specializing in Economic History.

189

TABLE 1. A. Entry Requirements and B. Degree Schemes

| | A. ENTRY REQUIREMENTS | | | | B. DEGREE SCHEMES | | | | | | | | | | |
| | None | Latin/Greek | Modern Language | Maths, etc. | Single Honours | Combined with | | | | Integrated | Pass | Area Studies | Other | Econ. Hist. Honours | Econ. Hist. Combined |
						Social Sciences	Languages	Other Arts	Other						
ABERDEEN	✓	R	R		✓	✓	✓	✓	✓		✓			✓	✓
ABERYSTWYTH	✓	R	R		✓	✓		✓			✓		✓		
BANGOR		R	R		✓			✓							
BIRMINGHAM		Oᵐ	O	Oᵉ	✓	✓		✓	✓						
BRADFORD	✓		R												
BRISTOL		O	R		✓	✓	✓	✓	✓	✓	✓	✓	✓	✓	✓
CAMBRIDGE	✓		R		✓	✓				✓	✓	✓		✓	✓
CARDIFF	✓		O/A		✓						✓	✓			✓
DUNDEE	✓	O/A	A		✓						✓	✓			✓
DURHAM			R			✓	✓	✓		✓	✓		✓	✓	✓
EAST ANGLIA (Eng. & Am.)			O/A*												
EAST ANGLIA (European)			O												
EDINBURGH		R	R		✓		✓		✓	✓					
ESSEX	✓														
EXETER	✓	O	R		✓	✓	✓	✓		✓	✓	✓	✓	✓	✓
GLASGOW		O		Oᵉ	✓	✓	✓	✓	✓	✓		✓	✓		✓
HERIOT-WATT															
HULL	✓	R	R		✓	✓	✓	✓	✓			✓			
KEELE	✓		O	Oᵉ	✓	✓	✓	✓				✓	✓	✓	✓
KENT		O	R	Oᵉ	✓	✓	✓	✓		✓		✓			✓
LANCASTER	✓		R		✓	✓	✓	✓		✓		✓		✓	✓
LEEDS	✓		O		✓	✓	✓	✓							
LEICESTER		O			✓	✓	✓	✓				✓			
LIVERPOOL		O		Oᵉ	✓	✓	✓	✓	✓	✓	✓	✓	✓	✓	✓

* Only for a three-year course.

190

TABLE 1 — *continued*

| | A. ENTRY REQUIREMENTS | | | | B. DEGREE SCHEMES | | | | | | | | | | |
	None	Latin/Greek	Modern Language	Maths, etc.	Single Honours	Combined with Social Sciences	Combined with Languages	Combined with Other Arts	Combined with Other	Integrated	Pass	Area Studies	Other	Econ. Hist. Honours	Econ. Hist. Combined
LONDON (External)		O / A^m	O / O^c/A^c		✓✓		✓	✓	✓		✓✓	✓✓		✓	✓
LONDON (Internal)		O		O	✓		✓	✓			✓	✓	✓		
LOUGHBOROUGH				A	✓	✓				✓					
MANCHESTER	✓		R / A/O		✓✓✓	✓	✓	✓	✓		✓✓	✓			✓
U.M.I.S.T.		O / A/O	A/O / R		✓✓✓	✓✓	✓	✓✓	✓		✓✓	✓✓	✓✓✓	✓	✓✓✓
NEWCASTLE	✓	O/A	O/A^c A^c R O/A^c	A/O	✓✓	✓✓	✓✓	✓✓✓	✓✓✓		✓	✓	✓✓✓	✓✓	✓✓✓
NOTTINGHAM	✓	R O O/A^m	A^c R		✓✓	✓✓	✓	✓✓✓	✓✓✓					✓	✓✓
OXFORD															
QUEEN'S, BELFAST															
READING															
SALFORD															
SHEFFIELD															
SOUTHAMPTON		R	A^c R	O/A	✓✓✓	✓✓✓	✓✓✓	✓✓✓		✓	✓✓✓	✓✓✓	✓✓	✓✓	✓
ST. ANDREWS	✓✓			O^c											
ST. DAVIDS (Lampeter)					✓				✓	✓	✓			✓	✓
STIRLING															
STRATHCLYDE															
SURREY			A^c R		✓✓✓✓	✓✓✓✓	✓✓✓✓	✓✓	✓✓		✓	✓✓✓✓	✓✓	✓✓	✓
SUSSEX															
SWANSEA			O/A R		✓✓✓										✓
ULSTER															
WARWICK															
YORK															

TABLE 2. *Areas of Study*

University	Methodology	Ancient	Archaeology	Medieval	British	Irish, Scots, Welsh	Europe	European Nations	World	Colonial	Africa	Asia	North America	South America	Social/Economic	Political/Constitutional	Military/Diplomatic	Cultural/Ecclesiastical	History of Science/Technol.	Local
ABERDEEN	✓	✓		✓	✓	✓	✓	✓		✓	✓		✓		✓	✓	✓	✓	✓	
ABERYSTWYTH	✓		✓	✓	✓	✓	✓	✓	✓	✓	✓		✓		✓	✓	✓			
BANGOR		✓	✓	✓	✓	✓	✓			✓			✓			✓		✓		
BIRMINGHAM				✓	✓		✓				✓		✓			✓		✓		
BRADFORD		✓					✓						✓			✓		✓		
BRISTOL	✓			✓	✓		✓	✓		✓	✓	✓	✓			✓	✓	✓	✓	
CAMBRIDGE	✓	✓	✓	✓	✓	✓	✓	✓	✓			✓	✓			✓	✓	✓	✓	
CARDIFF	✓	✓	✓	✓	✓	✓	✓	✓					✓			✓	✓	✓		
DUNDEE			✓	✓	✓		✓						✓			✓		✓		
DURHAM	✓				✓		✓						✓	✓	✓	✓		✓		
EAST ANGLIA	✓	✓			✓		✓	✓		✓	✓	✓	✓		✓	✓	✓	✓	✓	
EDINBURGH		✓			✓	✓	✓	✓		✓	✓	✓	✓	✓	✓	✓	✓	✓	✓	
ESSEX					✓		✓	✓					✓		✓	✓		✓		
EXETER	✓	✓	✓	✓	✓	✓	✓	✓					✓		✓	✓		✓		
GLASGOW	✓				✓		✓	✓			✓		✓	✓		✓		✓		
HERIOT WATT	✓			✓	✓															
HULL	✓	✓		✓	✓	✓	✓	✓	✓	✓	✓	✓	✓	✓	✓	✓	✓	✓	✓	✓
KEELE	✓	✓		✓	✓	✓	✓	✓	✓	✓	✓	✓	✓	✓	✓	✓	✓	✓	✓	✓
KENT	✓	✓	✓	✓	✓	✓	✓	✓	✓	✓		✓	✓	✓	✓		✓	✓	✓	✓
LANCASTER		✓	✓	✓	✓	✓	✓	✓		✓	✓	✓	✓	✓	✓	✓	✓	✓	✓	✓
LEEDS		✓	✓	✓	✓	✓	✓	✓	✓	✓	✓	✓	✓		✓			✓	✓	
LEICESTER		✓	✓	✓	✓		✓			✓		✓	✓	✓	✓	✓	✓	✓	✓	
LIVERPOOL	✓	✓		✓	✓	✓	✓	✓	✓	✓	✓	✓	✓	✓	✓	✓	✓	✓	✓	✓

TABLE 2. — continued

	Methodology	Ancient	Archaeology	Medieval	British	Irish, Scots, Welsh	Europe	European Nations	World	Colonial	Africa	Asia	North America	South America	Social/Economic	Political/Constitutional	Military/Diplomatic	Cultural/Ecclesiastical	History of Science/Technol.	Local
LONDON (External)	✓	✓		✓	✓		✓	✓		✓	✓	✓	✓	✓		✓	✓	✓		
LONDON (Internal)		✓	✓	✓	✓		✓	✓		✓	✓	✓	✓	✓	✓	✓	✓	✓	✓	
L'BOROUGH			✓		✓✓		✓✓						✓✓		✓✓✓	✓✓✓✓✓		✓✓	✓	
MANCHESTER		✓		✓	✓✓✓		✓✓✓	✓	✓	✓			✓✓		✓✓✓	✓✓✓✓✓	✓	✓✓	✓	✓
U.M.I.S.T.		✓✓✓	✓	✓✓✓	✓✓✓	✓	✓✓✓✓✓✓	✓	✓	✓			✓✓	✓	✓	✓✓✓✓✓	✓	✓✓	✓	
NEWCASTLE	✓	✓		✓✓	✓✓		✓✓✓✓✓✓✓	✓	✓✓	✓			✓✓		✓	✓✓✓✓✓	✓	✓✓		✓
NOTTINGHAM																				
OXFORD		✓	✓	✓✓	✓✓✓✓✓✓	✓	✓✓✓✓✓✓✓✓✓	✓✓	✓✓	✓✓✓✓	✓	✓✓✓	✓✓✓✓✓✓	✓✓✓	✓	✓✓	✓✓✓	✓✓✓✓✓✓✓		
QUEENS, BELFAST		✓																		
READING																				
SALFORD	✓																			✓
SHEFFIELD		✓	✓	✓✓✓✓	✓✓✓✓✓✓	✓✓✓	✓✓✓✓✓✓✓✓✓	✓✓✓	✓	✓✓✓✓	✓	✓✓✓	✓✓✓✓✓✓	✓✓	✓✓✓✓✓✓✓✓✓	✓✓	✓✓	✓✓✓✓✓✓		
SOUTHAMPTON																				
ST. ANDREWS																				
ST. DAVIDS																				
STIRLING																				
STRATHCLYDE							✓												✓	
SURREY	✓				✓✓✓✓✓	✓✓	✓✓✓✓✓	✓✓✓✓✓✓	✓✓✓	✓✓✓✓	✓	✓✓	✓✓✓✓✓	✓✓	✓✓✓✓✓✓✓✓✓✓	✓✓✓	✓✓✓✓✓	✓	✓	✓
SUSSEX	✓	✓		✓✓	✓✓✓✓✓	✓✓	✓✓✓✓✓	✓✓✓✓✓✓	✓✓✓	✓✓✓✓	✓	✓✓	✓✓✓✓✓	✓✓	✓✓✓✓✓✓✓✓✓✓	✓✓✓	✓✓✓✓✓	✓		
SWANSEA	✓																			
ULSTER	✓✓✓																			
WARWICK	✓	✓		✓	✓✓✓✓✓	✓	✓✓✓✓✓	✓✓✓✓✓✓	✓✓✓	✓✓✓✓	✓✓✓	✓	✓✓✓✓✓	✓✓	✓✓✓✓✓✓✓✓✓	✓	✓✓✓✓✓	✓✓		✓
YORK																				

193

Table 2: Areas of Study

This attempts to indicate the areas of historical study in which each University specializes, so that students whose interest has been roused by one of the chapters in the book can see at a glance where the branch of history in question can be studied. Being a schematic guide the classifications adopted are fairly broad, so that a tick in one column can indicate several courses at differing levels. The classifications are more or less self-explanatory save that 'European nations' means the history of individual nations as opposed to general topics in European history, and 'Colonial' covers all topics on the history of overseas empires and institutions.

Table 3: Other Degree Schemes Involving History

A. *Honours Degrees*

C.N.A.A. Joint Honours
  Arts: Portsmouth Polytechnic
  Humanities: Woolwich Polytechnic
  Modern Studies (this includes Politics, History and Geography): Lancaster College of Technology (Coventry), Barking Regional College (subject to C.N.A.A. approval)
  B.Sc. (Econ.) Modern Economic History: Ealing Technical College
  Nottingham University Honours Fine Arts and History: Nottingham College of Art and Design

B. *General Degrees*

C.N.A.A. Arts
  Manchester College of Commerce
  Portsmouth Polytechnic

London University External General Arts
  Barking Regional College
  Birmingham College of Commerce
  Bolton Institute of Technology
  Bournemouth College of Technology
  Ealing Technical College

194

Kingston College of Technology
Liverpool College of Commerce
Newcastle-upon-Tyne Polytechnic
North Western Polytechnic
Nottingham Regional College of Technology
Oxford College of Technology
The Polytechnic, Wolverhampton

C. *The Open University*

The Open University began to accept applications from January 1970 for its first session. This will begin in January 1971 as the Open University intends to work by the calendar rather than by the academic year. Fuller details of the course structure than that provided here can be obtained from the Secretary, The Open University, Walton Hall, Walton, Bletchley, Bucks.

The University offers both the B.A. and the B.A. with Honours. In order to obtain a B.A. degree a student will have to obtain six credits and for a B.A. with Honours eight. Each credit is granted after successfully completing a course at one of four levels. A student who reads history as part of his degree will be expected to obtain two credits from amongst the Foundation Year courses, and the remainder from Second, Third and Fourth Level courses. These units can be drawn from a wide range, with many combinations being available.

The potential historian will begin by taking the Foundation Course in 'The Humanities' together with one other Foundation Course. This will be interdisciplinary and deal partly with problems of methodology (the history component being concerned with justifications for the study of history, problems of periodization, historical semantics, etc., and the relationship between literature and art and the social and historical context) leading to a number of case studies (drawn from all the arts disciplines), including one on industrialization in the nineteenth century. At the Second Level there will be three integrated 'period studies' : 'Renaissance and Reformation', 'The Age of Revolutions' and 'The Twentieth Century'. Eventually there will be a variety of third and fourth level courses in history, including a course on 'War and Society' (involving co-operation with social science) and a course on 'Sources and Historiography for Nineteenth and Twentieth-Century British History' involving a small research project—which will be regarded as essential to an Honours degree in History.

Appendix II

GUIDE TO GRADUATE COURSES AT UNIVERSITIES IN THE UNITED KINGDOM

This section attempts to list the growing number of higher degree courses which are based not solely on a thesis but on advanced coursework and a short dissertation. The qualifications awarded as a result of each course are listed here but it must be remembered that the same nomenclature can encompass widely differing regulations and admission requirements. As specialization and cross-disciplinary links are more common at this level than in undergraduate degree schemes the list has been extended to cover not only orthodox historical topics but also courses in cultural and social science fields which are either related directly to history in approach or which contain a certain element of history. Where the mere title of a course is vague or ambiguous some attempt is made to indicate the scope of the course. However, the following is only an indication of what courses are available and further details should be obtained from the Universities concerned. Many of these publish a separate graduate studies prospectus which will give information on higher degrees by research as well as those obtainable by examination. The following books will also be of use:

Schedule of Postgraduate Courses in the U.K. (Committee of Vice-Chancellors, 6th ed., 1969).

Directory of Postgraduate Courses and Opportunities (Cornmarket Press, 1969).

G. Kitson Clark, *Guide for Research Students Working on Historical Subjects* (Cambridge University Press, 2nd ed., 1968).

G. R. Elton and G. Kitson Clark, *Guide to Research Facilities in History in the Universities of Great Britain and Ireland* (Cambridge University Press, 2nd ed., 1965). *United Kingdom Postgraduate Awards* (Association of Commonwealth Universities, published every two years).

ABERDEEN

History (M.LITT.)
Medieval Studies (Diploma)
Revolutions in S.E. Asia 1941-60 (M.LITT.)

ABERYSTWYTH

Dark Age Britain (M.A.)
Palaeography and Archive Administration (Diploma and College Certificate)

BANGOR

Palaeography and Archive Administration (Diploma)
Welsh Studies (Diploma)

BIRMINGHAM

African Studies (M.A.)
Economic and Social History (M.SOC.SC.)
Foreign Relations of the United States of America (M.A.)
French History and Civilization in the First Half of the Nineteenth Century (M.A.)
Greek Regional Studies (M.A.)
Historical Studies (English Culture and Society in the Later Middle Ages) (M.A.)
Modern German Studies (M.A.)
Renaissance France (M.A.)
Roman Provincial Studies (M.A.)
Russian Literature and Society (M.A.)

BRISTOL

Late Roman Studies (M.A.)
Prehistoric cultures of the Aegean and Anatolia (M.A.)

CAMBRIDGE

Classical Archaeology (Diploma)
Historical Studies (i.e. methodology) (Diploma)
Prehistoric Archaeology (Certificate)
Slavonic Studies (Diploma)

CARDIFF

History (M.A.)
Palaeography (no examination, save for periods prior to 1700)

DURHAM

Anglo-Saxon Studies (Diploma)
Archaeology and Early History of Northern England (Diploma)
British Prehistoric Archaeology (Diploma)
Romano-British Studies (Diploma)

EAST ANGLIA

Advanced Art Historical Studies (M.A.)
Development of European Institutions since 1945 (M.A.)
Economic History (M.A.)
Evolution of Modern Societies since 1870 (M.A.)
Growth of the Welfare State (M.A.)
History and English Literature (M.A.)
Seventeenth-Century History (English, Dutch and Regional) (M.A.)
The European Economy (M.A.)

EDINBURGH

African Studies (Diploma and M.LITT.)
Arabic and Islamic Studies (Diplomas and M.LITT.)
History (M.LITT.)
History of Art (Diploma)
North American Studies (M.LITT.)

Scottish History (M.LITT.)
Scottish Studies (Diploma and M.LITT.)

ESSEX

History and Theory of Architecture (M.A.)
Latin American Government and Politics (M.A.)
Literature (M.A.)
Sociology of Latin America (M.A.)
Sociology of the U.S.S.R. (M.A.)
Soviet Government and Politics (M.A.)
U.S. Government and Politics (M.A.)

EXETER

History (M.A.)
History of Technology (M.A.)
History of the Atlantic Economy (M.A.)

GLASGOW

Classics (B.PHIL.)
Latin American Studies (B.PHIL.)
Modern Chinese Studies (B.PHIL.)
Social Studies (B.PHIL.)
Soviet Studies (B.PHIL.)

HULL

Commonwealth Studies (B.PHIL.)
Economic and Social History (B.PHIL.)
History (B.PHIL.)
Local Historical Studies (Diploma)
South East Asian Studies (B.PHIL.)

KEELE

Medieval Studies (M.A.)
U.S. History and Institutions (M.A.)
Victorian Studies (M.A.)

KENT

Classical Studies (M.A.)
Modern German Studies (M.A.)

LANCASTER

English Literature and Society, 1910-45 (M.A.)
Modern Social History (M.A.)
Russian and Soviet Studies (M.A.)
Social History and Education (M.A.)

LEEDS

Celtic Studies (Diploma)
Economic History (M.A.)
History and Philosophy of Science (Diploma)
Medieval Studies (M.A.)
Palaeography and Historical Criticism (No examination)
Russian Studies (M.A.)

LEICESTER

Classics (M.A.)
English Local History (M.A.)
Museum Studies (Certificate)
Victorian Studies (M.A.)

LIVERPOOL

Ancient History and Classical Archaeology (B.PHIL.)
Economic History (B.PHIL.)
French and History (B.PHIL.)
German Studies (B.PHIL.)
Latin American Studies (B.PHIL.)
Local History (B.PHIL.)
Medieval Studies (B.PHIL.)
Modern History (W. Africa and U.S.A.) (M.A.)
Prehistoric Archaeology (B.PHIL.)
Russian Studies (B.PHIL.)
Study of Records and Administration of Archives (Diploma)

o

LONDON

Chelsea College
History and Philosophy of Science (M.PHIL.)
Modern Social and Cultural Studies (Diploma)

Courtauld Institute
History of Dress (Certificate)
History of European Art (M.A.)

Imperial College
History of Science (Diploma and/or M.SC.)
History of Technology (Diploma and/or M.SC.)

Institute of Archaeology
Archaeology (many options) (Diploma/M.PHIL.)

Institute of Commonwealth Studies
Area Studies : The Commonwealth (M.A.)

King's College
History (Medieval) (M.A.) (with U.C.L.)
Imperial and Commonwealth History (M.A.)
War Studies (M.A. and Diploma)

London School of Economics
Economic History (M.A. or M.SC.)
International History (M.A. or M.SC.)

School of Slavonic and East European Studies
Area Studies (M.A.)
History (E. European and Russian) (M.A.)
Soviet Studies (M.A.)

School of Oriental and African Studies
Archaeology (various options) (Diploma)
Area Studies (African, Near Middle Eastern, S. Asian, S.E. Asian and Far Eastern) (M.A.)
Oriental and African History (many options) (M.A.)

University College
Ancient History (M.A.)
Archive Administration (Diploma and M.A.)
Area Studies (Latin America, U.S.A.) (M.A.)
Classical Archaeology (Diploma)
Egyptology (Diploma)

English with European History (M.A.)
History and Philosophy of Science (M.SC.)
History of Science (M.SC.)
United States (M.A.)
Western European Archaeology (Diploma)

Warburg Institute
Combined Historical Studies : The Renaissance (M.PHIL.)

Westfield
History (M.PHIL.)
History of Art (M.PHIL.)

LOUGHBOROUGH

German Area Studies (Diploma)

MANCHESTER

Conservation and Repair of Historic Buildings (M.A.)
European Romanticism (M.A.)
History (Ancient, Sixteenth and Seventeenth century, modern or social topics) (M.A.)
History and Organization of Education (M.ED.)
History of Science and Technology (Given in U.M.I.S.T.) (M.SC.)
History of Western Architecture (M.A.)
Late Victorian and Edwardian Society 1870-1914 (M.A.)
Medieval Studies (Diploma)

NEWCASTLE

Archaeology (M.PHIL.)
French Studies (M.A. and M.PHIL.)
German Studies (M.A. and M.PHIL.)
Latin American Studies (M.A. and M.PHIL.)
Norwegian Studies (M.A.)
Prehistoric and Roman Britain (M.PHIL.)
Swedish Studies (M.A.)

OXFORD

Ancient History (B.PHIL.)
Archaeology (various options) (Diploma)
Celtic Studies (Diploma)
European History (B.PHIL.)
History of Art (Diploma)
History of the Commonwealth (B.PHIL.)
History and Philosophy of Science (Diploma)
History of the United States (B.PHIL.)
Indian Studies (B.PHIL.)
Jewish Studies (B.PHIL.)
Latin America (B.PHIL.)
Mesopotamian Studies (B.PHIL.)
Modern Middle Eastern Studies (B.PHIL.)
Russian and Eastern Europe (B.PHIL.)
Slavonic Studies (Diploma)
Social Studies (Special Diploma)

QUEEN'S UNIVERSITY, BELFAST

History (M.A.)
History and Philosophy of Science (M.SC.)

READING

Contemporary European Studies (a variety of options including French studies, German, Italian and History) (M.A. or M.PHIL.)
Medieval Studies (M.A. and M.PHIL.)

SHEFFIELD

Ancient History (M.A.)
British Politics since the mid-nineteenth century (M.A.)
History (English and European) (M.A.)
Homeric and Mycenean Studies (M.A.)
Political Theory (M.A.)
Social and Economic History of Minority Groups (M.A.)
The English Industrial Revolution (M.A.)

SOUTHAMPTON

American Studies (M.A.)
Medieval Studies (M.A.)

ST. ANDREWS

Ancient History (M.LITT.)
Medieval History (M.LITT.)
Modern History (M.LITT.)
Modern Russian Studies (M.LITT.)

STRATHCLYDE

Economic History (M.LITT.)

SURREY

German Area Studies (Diploma)

SUSSEX

African Studies (M.A.)
American Studies (M.A.)
Contemporary European Studies (Europe since 1945) (M.A.)
French Literature (considered partly in relation to French history) (M.A.)
History (British and European and mainly social and economic) (M.A.)
History of Ideas (M.A.)
History, Philosophy and Social Studies in Science (M.SC.)
History and Theory of Art (M.A.)
International Relations (with options covering periods since 1930) (M.A.)
Russian Studies (M.A.)
Sociological Studies (including comparative studies of Revolution) (M.A.)
South East Asian Studies (M.A.)

SWANSEA

History (M.A.)
Russian and East European Studies (M.A.)

ULSTER

Contemporary International History (M.A.)

WARWICK

French Studies (M.A.)
Labour History (M.A.)
Renaissance Studies (M.A. or M.PHIL.)

YORK

Economics, Statistics and Economic History (B.PHIL.)
Medieval Studies (B.PHIL.)

Index

Acton, Lord, 25, 182
Aeneid, 35
Africa, 10-11, 94, 146, 159-72; art in, 165; independence period, 170-1; labour migration, 166-7; languages, 167-8; Portuguese records on, 164-5
African Political Systems, 167
Agrarian History of England, The, 100
Agrarian Problem in the Sixteenth Century, The, 88
Agricola, 30
Alexander the Great, 28
Alexander II, 93
America. *See* U.S.A.
Amis, Kingsley, 42
Ancient history, 27-40; literary sources, 29-34; source-material for, 28-34
Ancient History, (Grant), 27, 30, 39
Andrew Jackson (Ward), 138
Angels in Marble, 78
Anglo-Saxon Chronicle, 46-7
Anjou, House of, 53-4
Annales, 123
Anne, Queen, 65
Annual Bulletin of Historical Literature, 22
Anselm, Archbishop, 54
Anthropology, 48, 163-5, 167
Anti-Semitism, 125-7
Aquinas, Thomas, 178
Archaeology, 24, 28-30, 32-3, 46-7, 163-5
Archaeology and Place Names and History, 47

Archimedes, 178
Archives, 68; private, 96
Archives and Local History, 23
Argentina, 146, 156
Aristotelianism, 180, 184
Aristotle, 36, 63, 178
Ashley, Sir William, 87
Ashton, T. S., 87
Asia, 10-11, 94, 146, 159-72; art in, 165; independence period, 170-1; labour migration, 166-7; languages, 167-8
Athens, 27-8, 31, 34, 36, 38, 86
Aubrey, John, 68
Australasia, 169
Austria, 52, 120
Aylmer, G. E., 123

Bacon, Francis, 58, 178, 182, 184
Bagehot, Walter, 79
Bamford, Samuel, 24
Barlow, G., 41, 187
Barraclough, G., 11, 43, 53, 56, 115, 130
Barrès, 125
Baxter, R., 68
Bede, Venerable, 46, 86
Beer, S. H., 74
Belgium, 120, 121
Beloff, M., 43, 56
Bentham, Jeremy, 146
Bergson, H. L., 125
Bibliography of Historical Writings . . . 1940-1945, 22
Bibliography of Modern History, A, 22
Biographie Universelle, 23

207

Japan, 92-4, 162-3
Jargon, 26
Jarvis, R. C., 108-10
Java,161
John, King, 49, 53
Johnson, Samuel, 171
Jones, Gwyn, 46
Jones, Sir William, 171

Keesing's Contemporary Archives, 22
Kenyatta, Jomo, 171
Khayyam, Omar, 2
Kingsley, Mary, 171
Kipps, 20
Kitson Clark, G., 23, 197-8
Knowles, Dom David, 19-20, 25, 45
Koyré, Alexandre, 181

La Nauze, J. A., 23
Lancashire, 108-10
Land reform, 87
Landes, D. S., 182
Languages, problems of, 121-2
Larousse, 23
Latin America, 10, 62, 94, 119, 145-58; military governments in, 156-7; miscegenation in, 153-4; diversity of population, 149; revolutions in, 157-8; Wars of Independence, 149-50, 154
Latin language, 42-4, 55, 58
Laud, Archbishop, 68
Law and Opinion, (Dicey), 87
Lee, Miss Jennie, 6
Leibniz, G. W., 182
Le Patourel, J., 56
Levellers, 62
Levi-Strauss, Claude, 48, 56
Libraries, use of, 15-26
Life of Galileo, 176
Lima, 152
Lloyd George, David, 79
Local government records, 95-6
Local Historian, The, 107
Local history, 7, 101-14, 141-2, 167; sources, 101-6
London in Tudor times, 59
Long Parliament, 69
Louis VI, 52; XIV, 122
Lovejoy, A. O., 181, 182
Low Countries. *See* Netherlands
Lucky Jim, 42

Ludlow, Edmund, 68
Lunar Society, 180-1
Lunar Society of Birmingham, The, 180

Macaulay, Lord, 25, 86
McFarlane, K. B., 50, 56
McKenzie, Robert, 73, 78
Mackintosh, J. P., 73-4
Madagascar, 164
Magna Carta, 49
Maitland, F. W., 45
Making of the English Working Class, (Thompson), 77
Malawi, 168
Malaya, 161
Man on a Donkey, The, 20
Marlborough, 18
Marprelate, Martin, 68-9
Marx, Karl, 185
Marxism, 126-7, 185
May, Henry F., 138, 139, 144
Mboya, Tom, 170
Medieval Empire: Idea and Reality, The, 56
Medieval English Borough, The, 19
Medieval history, 41-56, 90-1, 145
Medievalism, 42-5
Meiji, Emperor, 93
Memoirs, politicians', 83-4
Mexico, 146, 152; revolution in, 157
Mexico City, 152
Meyer, John R., 136
Michaud, 23
Middle Ages, 41-56, 60-2, 169
Military revolutions, 65
Mill, James, 160
Mill, J. S., 14, 79
Millar, John, 87
Milne, A. M., 22-3
Milton, John, 2, 58, 69
Missionaries, 160-1
Modena, 120
Modern British Politics, (Beer), 74
Modern English Usage, 20
Modern history, early, 57-70
Montaigne, 181
Montesquieu, 184
Monteverdi, 58
More, Sir Thomas, 58, 68
Music, 58
Mussolini, Benito, 126
Mycenae, 29

214